Invest With Confidence: For Black Women

By Michaela Dosunmu

Disclaimer:

The information contained in this book is for educational and informational purposes only. It is not intended as a substitute for professional advice, whether medical, psychological, financial, or otherwise. The author is not a licensed healthcare or mental health professional. Readers should seek advice from their physician, therapist, or other qualified professionals for any personal concerns related to health, habits, or behavior change.

While the practices and techniques discussed in this book are based on research and the author's experiences, individual results may vary. The recommendations in this book should be considered complementary to conventional medical, psychological, or professional care, and not as a replacement.

The author and publisher disclaim any liability for any direct or indirect consequences arising from the use of the information in this book. It is essential to consult with a qualified professional before implementing any significant lifestyle or behavioral changes, especially if you have a medical condition or specific personal circumstances.

By reading this book, you acknowledge that the information is not intended to diagnose or treat any condition and is provided on an "as-is" basis.

Table Of Contents

Introduction

This book, Invest with Confidence - For Black Women, helps you understand how to make smart decisions with your money. Investing might sound complicated, but it doesn't have to be. In fact, anyone can invest—even if you're starting with a small amount or don't know much about money yet. This book is here to guide you step by step, so you can feel confident about growing your money and building a secure future.

The first thing to know is that investing isn't only for wealthy people or financial experts. It's a way for anyone to make their money work for them over time. Investing is like planting a tree. You start with a small seed, and with time and patience, it grows into something valuable. Just like that, small amounts of money invested today can grow into something big in the future. The goal of this book is to help you understand how to start, what to invest in, and how to stick with it, so you can reach your financial goals. We will cover different ways to invest, like in stocks, bonds, and real estate. You'll learn how to set clear goals, whether it's saving for a home, college, retirement, or even a dream vacation. With a good plan and the right tools, you can reach those goals, even if you're starting small.

One important focus of this book is to encourage Black women to invest and build wealth. In the United States, many Black women face extra challenges when it comes to building financial security. This book aims to show you how to overcome those barriers and create a strong foundation for yourself and future generations. By investing, you're not only building wealth but also creating a legacy that can support your children, grandchildren, and beyond.

As you go through each chapter, you'll also find tips to help you feel confident with your money. Many people feel nervous or unsure about investing because they're afraid of making mistakes. But remember, everyone starts somewhere, and it's okay to learn along the way. This book will give you the knowledge and confidence to make smart choices without feeling overwhelmed. Small steps, like setting up a savings account or choosing your first investment, are what lead to bigger achievements. Investing takes patience and a steady approach, but the rewards are worth it. Imagine having enough money saved to reach your goals and enjoy life without worrying about finances.

Chapter 1

The Power of Investing

What is Investing?

Investing is when you use your money to make more money over time. Think of investing like planting a seed. When you plant it, care for it, and let it grow, it can become a strong tree that gives you fruit. Investing works similarly. You start with a small amount of money, put it in something that can grow (like stocks, bonds, or property), and let it build value over time. When you invest, you're not spending your money to buy something you'll use right away. Instead, you're putting it into something that has the potential to grow. This way, over time, the value of what you invested in can increase, giving you more than what you started with. People invest in things like companies, houses, or land because they believe these can increase in worth. Investing is a way to grow wealth because, if done wisely, it helps your money grow by earning more money on top of what you already have.

For example, imagine you buy one share in a company. Over time, if that company does well, the value of that share can increase. You could sell it for more than you paid, making a profit. This extra money you made is called a "return." Investing is powerful because it's one of the best ways to turn small amounts of money into larger amounts without having to work for every dollar gained.

Why is Investing Powerful?

Investing is powerful because it helps people achieve big goals. With investing, you don't have to rely only on the money you make from working. Instead, you set aside some money that keeps growing on its own. Over time, with the right investments, people can save for things like college, a new house, or retirement.

Here's an example of why investing is so powerful: imagine you save $100 and put it in a safe place at home. After 10 years, you still have $100. But if you invest that same $100 in something that grows 5% each year, you'd have more than $162 after 10 years. Even though you didn't add any more money, the original amount you invested increased because of the power of "growth." This growth comes from choosing investments that gain value over time.

The Difference Between Saving and Investing

It's important to understand that saving and investing are two different things, but both are helpful for your financial future.

Saving

When you save, you're putting money aside for safekeeping. You might put it in a bank account where it stays safe and can be used whenever you need it. Savings accounts usually don't grow your money very much, but they give you quick access to your cash. Saving is great for short-term goals or emergencies, like if you need money for unexpected bills or a small purchase.

Investing

Investing is about letting your money grow over time. Instead of putting it somewhere for safekeeping, you put it in something that has the potential to grow, like stocks or real estate. Investing carries more risk than saving because the value of investments can go up or down. However, with time and wise choices, investing can provide much bigger returns than saving.

When we talk about "risk" in investing, it means there's a chance that you might not make money—or could even lose some money—because investments can go down as well as up. But there's also a reward with investing, which means there's a chance your money will grow and give you much more in return. This is called "risk vs. reward."

Understanding Risk vs. Reward

Risk

In investing, risk is the chance that your money could lose value. For example, if you buy a share of a company, the value of that share might go down if the company has a bad year. While this can be scary, risk is a normal part of investing.

Reward

The reward is the extra money you make if your investment grows in value. For example, if you buy a share of a company and its value goes up, you can sell it for a higher price than you paid, making a profit.

Understanding the balance between risk and reward is important. Investments that have higher risks often offer the chance for higher rewards, but they also have a bigger chance of losing value. On the other hand, low-risk investments, like government bonds, don't give big returns but are safer.

How to Manage Risk

One way to manage risk is to not put all your money in one place. This is called "diversification." By spreading your investments across different things, like stocks, bonds, and maybe real estate, you lower the chance of losing money all at once. For example, if one investment goes down, another one might go up, balancing your overall growth.

Why Black Women Should Invest

The Wealth Gap and How Investing Can Help

The "wealth gap" is the difference in money and property that different groups of people own. In the United States, studies have shown that Black families often have less wealth than White families, and this gap can make it harder to reach big life goals, like buying a home or retiring comfortably. For Black women, who face both gender and racial challenges, this wealth gap is even wider.

Why the Wealth Gap Exists

The roots of the wealth gap are deeply tied to historical and systemic barriers. Here's an overview of some key factors that have contributed to this disparity:

1. Slavery and Historical Oppression

The legacy of slavery in the United States stripped generations of Black families of opportunities to build wealth. Enslaved people were denied ownership of property, education, and financial resources, and even after emancipation, systemic barriers like segregation and discrimination persisted. These limitations created a significant disadvantage in wealth accumulation compared to White families.

2. Racial Discrimination in Housing

Policies like redlining, which was prevalent from the 1930s through the 1970s, prevented Black families from buying homes in certain neighborhoods or accessing mortgages. Since homeownership is a primary way families build wealth in the U.S., these policies significantly impacted Black communities. Even today, the effects of these discriminatory practices linger, with Black households owning homes at much lower rates than White households.

3. Immigration and Economic Exclusion

Black immigrants and their descendants have also faced systemic barriers in accessing economic opportunities. Many came to the U.S. seeking a better life, but they were often relegated to low-paying jobs with limited upward mobility. This, combined with racial discrimination, hindered wealth-building opportunities.

4. The Gender Pay Gap

Black women face a dual disadvantage due to both racial and gender pay gaps. According to recent data (2020–2025), Black women earn about 63 cents for every dollar earned by White, non-Hispanic men. This income disparity reduces the ability to save, invest, and build wealth over time.

5. Limited Access to Financial Education

Black communities have historically had less access to financial education and tools, limiting opportunities for wealth accumulation. Many Black women grow up without exposure to investment strategies or financial planning resources, further widening the gap.

How Investing Can Help

Investing provides an opportunity to break this cycle and create pathways for financial empowerment. By participating in the stock market, real estate, and other wealth-building opportunities, Black women can:

- Grow their income beyond wages.
- Build generational wealth to pass down to their families.
- Gain financial independence and security to overcome systemic barriers.

Financial Independence and Security

Financial independence means being able to take care of yourself without relying on others for money. For Black women, financial independence can be especially important. When you're financially independent, you have more control over your life. You can make choices about where to live, what to study, or what work to do without being held back by money worries.

Investing is a key step toward financial independence. By building wealth through investments, Black women can create a safety net, a cushion of money that can help during tough times. For example, if you have investments, they can help cover costs if you lose a job or face unexpected expenses. The growth from investments gives you extra support, making it easier to manage life's ups and downs.

Building Generational Wealth

"Generational wealth" means passing money, property, or valuable things from one generation to the next. If parents or grandparents can save and invest, they can leave that wealth to their children or grandchildren. This gives future generations a better starting point, helping them pay for things like college or buying a home.

For Black families, building generational wealth has been challenging because of historical barriers. But by investing, Black women can start building wealth that can be passed down. Even small investments today can grow over time, giving future generations a better chance at financial success. This means that by investing now, Black women are not only helping themselves but are also setting up a stronger financial future for their families.

Creating Economic Opportunities

Investing can also open doors to new opportunities. As investments grow, Black women can use their wealth to start businesses, buy property, or support causes they care about. These actions create jobs and resources for communities, making positive changes for more people. When Black women invest in their communities, they create opportunities that benefit others, helping to strengthen the community as a whole.

Overcoming Investment Myths

Myth 1: "Investing is Too Risky"

One of the biggest myths about investing is that it's "too risky," or that you're likely to lose all your money if you invest. While it's true that all investments come with some risk, not every investment is the same. Different types of investments have varying levels of risk, and some are much safer than others.

Current Investment Risk and Performance Statistics (2020–2025)

Stocks

- o The S&P 500, a benchmark for the U.S. stock market, delivered an average annual return of approximately 12% from 2020 to 2025, even including periods of volatility such as the steep decline during the COVID-19 pandemic in 2020.
- o During the pandemic, the market dropped by about 33% in March 2020, but it recovered within months, hitting all-time highs by the end of 2021.

- Growth stocks, particularly in technology, saw significant gains. For instance, companies like Apple (AAPL) and Microsoft (MSFT) had annualized returns of over 15% during this period.

Bonds

- U.S. Treasury Bonds, considered some of the safest investments, provided annual yields of 1.5% to 4.3% depending on the year and bond maturity, reflecting the fluctuating interest rate environment.
- Corporate bonds, which carry slightly more risk than government bonds, offered average annual returns of 4% to 6%. High-quality bonds remained a stable option for risk-averse investors, even during periods of market uncertainty.

Savings Accounts

- Traditional savings accounts offered minimal growth, with interest rates as low as **0.01% to 0.5%** from 2020 to 2022. However, high-yield savings accounts began offering **3% to 4%** annual interest by 2023–2025 due to rising interest rates, providing a safer but slower growth option for funds.

Real Estate

- Real estate investments, including rental properties, saw steady returns of 7% to 10% annually during this period, depending on the market. Urban areas experienced higher growth in housing prices due to increased demand.
- However, rising mortgage rates in 2023 and 2024, which peaked above **7%**, slowed the housing market in some regions, emphasizing the importance of choosing properties wisely.

Cryptocurrencies

- Cryptocurrencies, like Bitcoin, demonstrated extreme volatility. Bitcoin rose from $7,000 in early 2020 to over $60,000 in 2021 but also saw sharp declines, falling below $20,000 in 2022. By 2025, it stabilized in the range of $30,000 to $40,000.
- These investments offer high potential returns but are not suitable for everyone due to their unpredictability.

Balancing Risk with Safer Investments

On the other hand, some investments carry lower risks and provide steady growth:

Bonds

A safer choice than stocks, with consistent returns that provide income for investors.

Savings Accounts and CDs

Virtually risk-free, they are ideal for short-term savings or emergency funds but offer limited growth.

Myth 2: "You Need to Be Rich to Invest"

Another common myth is that you need a lot of money to start investing. This isn't true! Investing is not just for rich people. In fact, anyone can start with small amounts. Some people start investing with just a few dollars. Today, many apps and companies allow you to invest small amounts, even as low as $5 or $10.

There's also something called "fractional shares," which lets you buy just a small piece of a stock instead of a whole share. This way, if you want to invest in a big company like Amazon or Apple but can't afford one whole share, you can buy just a small piece of one. This makes investing possible even for those who don't have a lot of extra money.

Starting with small amounts also helps you learn without feeling scared about losing too much. You can see how investments work and feel more comfortable as you go. By starting small, you can build your confidence and, as your money grows, you may feel ready to invest a little more.

Addressing Fears and Building Confidence to Start Investing

Fears about investing often come from not knowing how it works or feeling like it's too complicated. Many people worry they will make a mistake or lose their hard-earned money. But with a little learning and practice, investing can become much less scary. Here are some ways to address these fears:

Learn the Basics First

Start by understanding the simple terms and ideas of investing. Know what stocks, bonds, mutual funds, and exchange-traded funds (ETFs) are. You don't need to know everything right away. Focus on learning step-by-step. Once you know what each type of investment does, you'll feel more confident about your choices.

Start Small

If you're worried about losing money, remember that you don't have to invest a large amount to begin. You can start with as little as $10 or even less. With a small investment, you can watch what happens and learn without feeling too stressed. Many people feel more confident after seeing their small investments grow, even just a little.

Ask for Help if You Need It

If you feel lost, don't be afraid to ask questions. There are many online resources, books, and even people who can help you learn about investing. Financial advisors or experienced investors can give advice if you're unsure. Talking to others can help clear up any confusion and make you feel more comfortable.

Remember That Mistakes Are Okay

Even experienced investors sometimes make mistakes. Not every investment will make money, and that's okay. The important thing is to learn from any mistakes. If you see that one investment didn't do well, you can use that knowledge to make better choices next time. Building wealth through investing is a long-term process, so small mistakes along the way are normal.

Focus on Your Goals

Think about why you want to invest. Are you saving for the future, for education, or to buy a home? Having a goal in mind can help you stay focused and feel motivated. When you know what you're working toward, you can stay steady, even when your investments go up and down.

Chapter 2

Setting Financial Goals For Investment Success

Why Financial Goals Matter

When you set a goal, it gives you something to work towards. It's like having a target to aim at. In the same way, setting financial goals helps you decide where you want your money to go and how you want it to grow. Investing without a goal is like driving without knowing where you're headed. Goals help make your investment choices clearer and give you a reason to stay committed, even if things get difficult.

Financial goals make investing feel more meaningful because they remind you of what you're trying to achieve. For example, if you're investing to save for college, you'll probably choose different investments than if you're saving for retirement. By having clear goals, you know what type of investments make sense for you and how much time you need to reach them. This way, your investments match your life plans.

Short-Term, Medium-Term, and Long-Term Goals

When it comes to financial goals, they can generally be divided into three types: short-term, medium-term, and long-term. Each type of goal is for a different amount of time, and knowing which is which helps you decide how to invest.

Short-Term Goals

What Are Short-Term Goals?

Short-term goals are things you want to achieve within a year or two. These are often simple goals, like saving for a vacation, buying a new phone, or building a small emergency fund in case of unexpected expenses.

Investing for Short-Term Goals

For short-term goals, it's important to keep your money safe. Since you'll need it soon, you don't want to take big risks that could make you lose money. Investing in safe places, like a savings account or a short-term bond, can be helpful. These don't grow as fast as other investments, but they keep your money safe and ready for when you need it. With short-term goals, the focus is on security rather than big growth.

Medium-Term Goals

What Are Medium-Term Goals?

Medium-term goals are usually set for about 3 to 5 years. These might be goals like saving for a down payment on a house, buying a car, or paying for a big event like a wedding. Medium-term goals are not as immediate as short-term goals, but you'll still need them sooner than retirement.

Investing for Medium-Term Goals

When investing for medium-term goals, you can take a little more risk than with short-term goals, but not too much. Investments like bonds, mutual funds, or a mix of safe and slightly riskier stocks can be a good choice. They give your money some time to grow but aren't as unpredictable as long-term investments. For example, you might invest in a bond that grows over a few years or put money into a balanced mutual fund, which has both stocks and bonds.

Long-Term Goals

What Are Long-Term Goals?

Long-term goals are goals you plan for 10, 20, or even 30 years down the line. Retirement is one of the most common long-term goals. Other long-term goals might include saving for your children's education or building a large fund to pass down to family members. Long-term goals are big and need more time to grow.

Investing for Long-Term Goals

For long-term goals, you can choose investments that have more potential for growth, even if they have more risk. This is because you have more time to ride out any ups and downs in the market. Stocks, real estate, or certain mutual funds can be good choices for long-term goals because they have the chance to grow a lot over time. By giving these investments more years, you give them time to increase in value, making it easier to reach your big goals.

Aligning Investments with Your Goals

Knowing which type of goal you're saving for—short, medium, or long-term—helps you choose the right investment. Here's how:

Match Time with Investment Type

If your goal is soon, like a year or two, stick with safe investments. This way, you won't lose money you need soon.

If your goal is a bit farther away, like 3–5 years, consider balanced investments. These let you grow your money but still offer some stability.

If your goal is far in the future, like 10 years or more, choose investments with growth potential, even if they have some risk.

Keep Checking Your Progress

As you invest, check regularly to see if you're on track. If your goals or timelines change, you may need to adjust your investments.

Stay Focused on Your Goal

Keeping your goal in mind can help you stay calm when investments go up and down. Knowing why you're investing makes it easier to stay patient, even if things are slow.

Creating a Personal Investment Plan

Steps to Develop a Personalized Investment Strategy

Creating a personal investment plan means making a clear and simple guide for how you want to invest your money. This plan helps you know what to invest in, how much to put in, and when you should start. Here's how to make an investment plan that fits your life and your goals:

Set Your Financial Goals

The first step is to decide what you're saving and investing for. Do you want to buy a car in a few years, or are you planning for retirement? Knowing your goals gives your plan direction. It also helps you choose the right types of investments. Goals can be short-term (1-2 years), medium-term (3-5 years), or long-term (10+ years).

Decide How Much You Can Invest

Look at your budget and see how much money you can set aside each month or each year for investing. It doesn't have to be a lot; even a small amount can grow over time. The important part is to start and keep adding to your investments regularly.

Choose Your Investment Types

Different goals need different types of investments. For example:

For short-term goals, you might use a savings account or bonds, which are safe.

For medium-term goals, you could pick a mix of stocks and bonds.

For long-term goals, you might choose more stocks, which have a higher chance of growth over time.

By matching the right investments with each goal, you're making a plan that's easy to follow and more likely to help you reach your goals.

Decide How Often to Add to Your Investment

Many people invest regularly, like every month or every few months. This is called "dollar-cost averaging," where you add money to your investments at regular times. Doing this can help you avoid worrying about market changes since you'll be investing over time, not just all at once.

Review and Adjust Your Plan

Every few months or at least once a year, look at your plan. Check if you're on track to reach your goals. If something changes, like a new job, family expenses, or a big life event, you might need to adjust your plan. Reviewing your plan regularly helps you stay focused and make small adjustments if needed.

Determining Your Risk Tolerance and Timeline for Investing

Before you start investing, it's important to understand how much risk you're comfortable with. This is called "risk tolerance." Your risk tolerance and the timeline for your goals will guide you in choosing investments that make sense for you.

Understanding Risk Tolerance

What is Risk Tolerance?

Risk tolerance is the amount of risk you're willing to take with your money. Some people are okay with taking big risks for the chance of bigger rewards, while others prefer safer choices, even if they grow slower. Knowing your risk tolerance helps you pick investments that feel comfortable.

How to Figure Out Your Risk Tolerance

Think About Your Comfort Level

If the idea of losing money makes you nervous, you may want safer investments like bonds. These grow slowly but are usually more stable. But if you're okay with some ups and downs for the chance of making more money, you might be fine with more stocks in your portfolio.

Consider Your Financial Situation

If you're saving for something important that you need soon, you might want lower-risk investments. But if you have extra money and won't need it for a long time, you might feel okay with riskier choices since you have more time to recover if there's a loss.

Determining Your Investment Timeline

What is an Investment Timeline?

An investment timeline is the length of time you plan to keep your money invested. Each goal has its own timeline, and this affects how you invest.

How to Match Timeline with Risk

Short-Term Timeline (1-2 years)

For short-term goals, like a vacation or a small purchase, choose safer investments because you need the money soon. Safe options, like savings accounts or bonds, can protect your money from big losses.

Medium-Term Timeline (3-5 years)
For medium-term goals, you have more time, so you can take a little more risk. A mix of stocks and bonds can help grow your money without too much ups and downs.
Long-Term Timeline (10+ years)
For long-term goals, like retirement or saving for a child's education, you can take more risk because you have time to wait through any market ups and downs. Stocks, which are riskier but grow more over time, are good for these goals.

Bringing It All Together

By knowing your goals, your comfort with risk, and your timeline, you can build a personalized investment plan. This plan will help guide your decisions so you know exactly how much to invest, where to put your money, and what steps to take to reach your goals. As you follow your plan, you'll see how each decision fits your big picture, making it easier to stay focused and motivated.

Financial Literacy for Investors

When starting to invest, understanding some key financial terms and concepts can help you feel more confident. Knowing these ideas can help you make smarter decisions and understand how your money is growing. Here are some of the most important terms every investor should know.

Return on Investment (ROI)

What is ROI?

Return on Investment, or ROI, shows how much money you make compared to how much you invested. It's a way to see if your investment is doing well or not. If your ROI is positive, you made money; if it's negative, you lost money.

How to Calculate ROI

Correct ROI Formula:
ROI= (profit/cost of investment) ×100

Steps to Calculate ROI:

1. Find the Profit:

Profit = Final Value of Investment - Initial Cost of Investment

2. Divide the Profit by the Initial Cost of Investment.
3. Multiply by 100 to convert it into a percentage.

Example:

- Initial Investment: $1,000
- Final Value of Investment: $1,200
- Profit: $1,200 - $1,000 = $200

ROI – (200/1000) ×100-20%

This means the investment yielded a 20% return.

Diversification

What is Diversification?

Diversification is a strategy to spread your money across different types of investments. The idea is "don't put all your eggs in one basket." By having a mix of investments, you reduce the risk of losing money all at once. For example, instead of putting all your money in stocks, you might put some in bonds, real estate, or other assets. This way, if one investment loses value, the others may still do well.

Why Diversification Matters

Diversification helps protect your investments from big losses. If one type of investment has a bad year, your other investments might still grow or stay stable, balancing things out.

Compound Interest

What is Compound Interest?

Compound interest means earning interest on both the money you invest and the interest you've already earned. It's like a snowball effect, where the interest you earn keeps adding up over time.

How Compounding Works

Imagine you invest $100 at 5% interest per year. In the first year, you earn $5. In the second year, you earn interest on $105, so you make a little more.

Over many years, compounding can help your investment grow a lot faster than simple interest, which only earns on the original amount.

Risk and Reward

What is Risk?

Risk is the chance of losing money on an investment. Every investment has some level of risk. For example, stocks can go up and down in value, so they're riskier. But some things, like savings accounts, have very little risk because they don't change in value as much.

What is Reward?

Reward is the potential gain from an investment. Often, higher-risk investments have the potential for higher rewards, but they can also lose value more easily. Lower-risk investments grow slower but are usually safer.

Asset Allocation

What is Asset Allocation?

Asset allocation means deciding how to spread your money across different types of investments, like stocks, bonds, and cash. The way you allocate, or divide, your money depends on your goals, your timeline, and how much risk you're comfortable with.

Why Asset Allocation Helps

By allocating your assets in different places, you create a balanced investment plan. For example, if you're young and saving for retirement, you might put more in stocks because you have time to handle ups and downs. But if you need the money sooner, you might choose safer investments like bonds.

Knowing these terms—ROI, diversification, compound interest, risk and reward, and asset allocation—can help you make smart investment choices. These are basic ideas that guide how your money grows and how you can manage it wisely. Understanding them will give you a strong foundation as you start investing.

Chapter 3

Understanding Different Types of Investments

Stocks

Stocks are one of the most popular ways to invest and grow your money. Let's explore what stocks are, how they work, and how to buy and sell them.

What Are Stocks?

A stock is a small part, or "share," of a company. When you buy a stock, you own a tiny piece of that company. Think of it like a pizza. Each slice represents a part of the whole pizza. When you buy one slice, you own that part. Similarly, if a company has one million shares and you buy one share, you own one-millionth of that company.

Companies sell stocks to raise money for things like building new products, expanding their business, or paying for research. When you buy a share of stock, you're helping the company by providing money they can use to grow. In return, you become a part-owner of the company and have a chance to earn money if the company does well.

How Stocks Grow Your Wealth

There are two main ways stocks can grow your money: *stock price increases* and *dividends.*

Stock Price Increases

When a company does well, more people want to buy its stock, which makes the stock price go up. For example, if you buy a stock for $10 and later its price rises to $15, you can sell it and make a profit of $5. The more the company grows and performs well, the higher its stock price can go. However, if the company doesn't do well, the stock price might go down, and you could lose money if you sell at a lower price.

Dividends

Some companies pay a small amount of money, called a dividend, to their stockholders as a way of sharing their profits. Not all companies pay dividends, but many larger, stable companies do. For example, if you own a stock that pays a $1 dividend per share each year, and you have 10 shares, you'd get $10 every year just for holding those shares. Dividends provide a steady income from your investment, even if the stock price doesn't change. Both stock price increases and dividends can help you grow your wealth over time.

Introduction to Stock Exchanges

Stocks are bought and sold on special places called "stock exchanges." A stock exchange is like a marketplace where people buy and sell shares. The two biggest stock exchanges in the United States are the New York Stock Exchange (NYSE) and the NASDAQ.

When a company "goes public," it lists its shares on an exchange. This means anyone can buy or sell its shares on that exchange. Companies are listed by symbols, like "AAPL" for Apple or "MSFT" for Microsoft. People use these symbols to find the company they want to buy or sell.

The price of a stock on an exchange can go up or down throughout the day. This change happens because of *supply and demand.* If more people want to buy a stock, the price goes up. If more people want to sell, the price goes down.

How to Buy and Sell Stocks

Buying and selling stocks is easier than ever today. Here's a simple step-by-step on how it works:

1. Open an Investment Account

To buy and sell stocks, you'll need a brokerage account. A brokerage account is like a bank account but is used for investing. Many companies, like Robinhood, E*TRADE, Fidelity, and Charles Schwab, allow you to open an account online. Some accounts even let you start with a small amount of money.

2. Deposit Money in Your Account

After opening an account, deposit money into it. This is the money you'll use to buy stocks.

3. Choose the Stocks You Want to Buy

Research the companies you're interested in. Look at things like their earnings, growth, and how well they've performed over time. Most people start with well-known companies they believe will keep growing.

High Performers in the Last 20 Years

Here are some of the most consistently high-performing stocks over the past two decades:

Apple Inc. (AAPL)

Known for its innovative products like the iPhone and MacBook, Apple has been one of the most valuable and profitable companies in the world. Its stock price has grown dramatically since the early 2000s.

Amazon.com Inc. (AMZN)

Starting as an online bookstore, Amazon has grown into a global e-commerce giant. Its stock has seen tremendous growth due to its dominance in retail, cloud computing (AWS), and technology.

Microsoft Corporation (MSFT)

A leader in software, cloud computing, and enterprise solutions, Microsoft has shown consistent growth, especially with its focus on cloud services like Azure.

Alphabet Inc. (GOOGL)

The parent company of Google, Alphabet dominates online search, advertising, and YouTube, making it a favorite among investors.

Tesla Inc. (TSLA)

Tesla has revolutionized the electric vehicle market and renewable energy. Its stock has skyrocketed in recent years due to increasing demand for EVs and innovative energy solutions.

NVIDIA Corporation (NVDA)

A leading company in graphics processing units (GPUs) and artificial intelligence, NVIDIA has been a top performer in the technology sector.

Berkshire Hathaway (BRK.A and BRK.B)

Led by Warren Buffett, this company invests in diverse businesses and has shown consistent returns over decades.

Netflix Inc. (NFLX)

Known for its streaming services, Netflix has transformed the entertainment industry and delivered strong stock performance as it expanded globally.

Johnson & Johnson (JNJ)

A healthcare giant, Johnson & Johnson has delivered steady returns, benefiting from its diversified portfolio of medical devices, pharmaceuticals, and consumer health products.

Place an Order

When you're ready to buy, you place an "order" through your brokerage account. This tells the exchange you want to buy a certain number of shares at the current price. If someone is selling shares, the trade happens, and the shares appear in your account.

Hold or Sell Your Stocks

Once you own shares, you can keep them as long as you want, hoping they'll go up in value. If they reach a price you're happy with, you can sell them to make a profit. You simply place a "sell order" on your brokerage account, and when someone buys your shares, the money goes back to your account.

Bonds

What Are Bonds?

Bonds are like loans that you give to organizations, such as the government or a company. When you buy a bond, you're lending your money to that organization for a set period. In return, they promise to pay you back with a bit of extra money, called interest. Think of it as lending money to a friend who says they'll pay you back plus a little extra as a thank-you.

Bonds are considered lower-risk investments compared to stocks. This means they are generally safer, and you're less likely to lose your money. While bonds don't usually grow your money as fast as stocks might, they provide a steady and reliable way to earn income over time. This makes bonds a good choice if you want to invest without taking on too much risk.

How Bonds Work

When you buy a bond, you are agreeing to lend your money for a certain amount of time, known as the "term" of the bond. This term might be a few months or many years, depending on the bond. In exchange, the organization that issued the bond pays you interest, usually every six months or once a year. When the term ends, the organization pays back the full amount you originally invested. Here's how it works:

You Buy the Bond

For example, let's say you buy a bond for $1,000 with a 3% interest rate and a 10-year term. The organization will pay you 3% of $1,000, or $30, each year as interest.

You Earn Interest During the Term

Each year, you receive $30 as interest. Over 10 years, that adds up to $300.

Getting Your Money Back

After 10 years, when the bond term ends, the organization pays you back the original $1,000.

This steady interest makes bonds a dependable choice, especially for people who want regular income from their investments without much risk.

Types of Bonds

There are different types of bonds, and each type is issued by a different kind of organization. The three main types are government bonds, corporate bonds, and municipal bonds. Each type of bond has different levels of safety and risk.

Government Bonds

Government bonds are bonds issued by the federal government. In the United States, these bonds are called Treasury bonds (or T-bonds for short). Since they are backed by the government, they are usually considered the safest type of bond.

Why Are Government Bonds Safe?

The government is unlikely to fail to pay back its debt, so people trust these bonds as a very low-risk investment. Because they're so safe, the interest rate on government bonds is usually lower than on other types of bonds. People who want a secure investment often choose government bonds, even though they don't make as much money as other, riskier investments.

Corporate Bonds

Corporate bonds are bonds issued by companies. When a company wants to raise money, it might issue bonds to investors. For example, if a company needs money to build a new factory, it might sell bonds to investors and pay them back with interest over time.

Are Corporate Bonds Risky?

Corporate bonds are riskier than government bonds because there's a chance the company could face financial problems. If a company goes out of business, it might not be able to pay back bondholders. However, most companies that issue bonds are stable and trustworthy. The level of risk depends on the company's financial health; larger, established companies are less risky than newer, smaller ones.

Why Choose Corporate Bonds?

Corporate bonds usually offer a higher interest rate than government bonds because they come with a little more risk. People who want more return on their investment and are okay with taking a bit more risk might choose corporate bonds.

Municipal Bonds

Municipal bonds are bonds issued by local governments, like cities, towns, or states. These bonds help pay for projects that benefit the community, such as building schools, hospitals, roads, or parks.

How Safe Are Municipal Bonds?

Municipal bonds are generally safe, but their risk depends on the financial health of the issuing city or state. Large cities with stable finances are more reliable than smaller towns with fewer resources. Still, municipal bonds are considered safer than corporate bonds but riskier than government bonds.

What's Special About Municipal Bonds?

One advantage of municipal bonds is that the interest earned is often exempt from federal income taxes. In some cases, if you buy bonds from your state, the interest might be free from state taxes, too. This tax advantage makes municipal bonds appealing, especially to people in higher tax brackets who want to save on taxes.

Mutual Funds and ETFs

What Are Mutual Funds and ETFs?

Mutual funds and ETFs (Exchange-Traded Funds) are types of investments that allow you to pool your money with other people. Imagine a basket that holds different types of investments, like stocks, bonds, or even real estate. When you buy a share of a mutual fund or ETF, you own a small piece of everything in that basket.

These funds are managed by experts who decide what investments to put in the basket, keeping track of them daily. Instead of having to pick each stock or bond yourself, mutual funds and ETFs make it easy by giving you access to many different investments with just one purchase. This can be very helpful if you're new to investing because you get a mix of investments without having to study each one on your own.

Why Are They Great for Beginners?

Simplicity

Mutual funds and ETFs are simple to use because they let you own a variety of investments in one go. For beginners, this makes investing easier. Instead of spending time choosing and buying individual stocks or bonds, you can buy a fund and immediately own many different investments.

Professional Management

When you invest in a mutual fund or ETF, a team of professionals manages the money for you. These experts decide which stocks or bonds to buy or sell in the fund. This professional management can give you peace of mind, knowing your investment is being handled by people who know the market well.

Affordable to Start

Mutual funds and ETFs can be affordable, and you don't need a lot of money to start. Some funds let you invest with small amounts, which makes it easy for beginners to get started. ETFs, in particular, can be purchased like stocks, so you can buy one share at a time, often for a lower cost. Here are some examples of easy-to-purchase mutual funds and ETFs that are beginner-friendly:

Easy-to-Purchase Mutual Funds

1. Vanguard Target Retirement Fund

These funds are designed for retirement savings and automatically adjust their risk levels as you approach your target retirement date. You can start with a low initial investment (e.g., $1,000 for most accounts) and benefit from professional management.

2. Fidelity ZERO Index Funds

Fidelity offers a series of no-expense-ratio mutual funds, such as the Fidelity ZERO Total Market Index Fund (FZROX) or Fidelity ZERO International Index Fund (FZILX). These funds require no minimum investment and have no management fees, making them great for first-time investors.

3. T. Rowe Price Blue Chip Growth Fund (TRBCX)

This mutual fund focuses on large, established companies with growth potential. While the minimum investment requirement may vary, it's considered a good option for beginners looking for stable growth.

Easy-to-Purchase ETFs

1. SPDR S&P 500 ETF Trust (SPY)

This ETF tracks the performance of the S&P 500 index, which includes 500 of the largest companies in the United States. It's one of the most popular ETFs and can be purchased with the price of one share.

2. iShares Core MSCI Total International Stock ETF (IXUS)

This ETF provides exposure to international stocks from both developed and emerging markets. It's a cost-effective way to diversify globally with just one purchase.

3. Vanguard Total Stock Market ETF (VTI)

This ETF gives investors access to the entire U.S. stock market, including large, medium, and small companies. With no minimum investment beyond the cost of a single share, it's an excellent choice for beginners.

4. Schwab U.S. Broad Market ETF (SCHB)

This ETF offers a low-cost option to invest in a wide range of U.S. stocks. It's ideal for beginners seeking affordable diversification.

5. Invesco QQQ Trust (QQQ)

This ETF focuses on the largest non-financial companies listed on the NASDAQ, often tech-heavy. It's a favorite among investors looking to include high-growth tech companies in their portfolio.

How Do They Help Diversify Your Portfolio?

How Mutual Funds and ETFs Diversify Your Portfolio

When you buy a mutual fund or ETF, you're automatically investing in a variety of stocks, bonds, or other assets. For example, a mutual fund might include stocks from 50 or even 100 different companies. An ETF could contain stocks from an entire industry or country. This variety means you're not putting all your money in one place. If one stock goes down, other stocks in the fund may still do well, helping to balance things out.

Types of Funds for Different Goals

Stock Funds: These focus on shares in companies and are good if you want higher growth.

Bond Funds: These focus on bonds, offering safer growth but with less return.

Balanced Funds: These mix stocks and bonds for moderate growth and risk.

By choosing funds that fit your goals, you get a diversified portfolio that can grow steadily.

Real Estate

Overview of Investing in Real Estate

Real estate is a type of investment where you buy property or land. There are different ways to invest in real estate, including rental properties, REITs, and home ownership. Let's take a closer look at each option.

Rental Properties

Rental properties are homes, apartments, or buildings that you buy and rent out to others. The people who live there, called tenants, pay you rent every month. The information with general global or U.S. statistics, I can provide an update based on verified sources:

In the United States, approximately 36% of households are renters, according to the U.S. Census Bureau's 2022 data. This equates to around 44 million rental households, showing a significant demand for rental properties nationwide.

This rent becomes a steady income for you. Owning rental properties can be a good way to make money regularly, but it does take time and effort to manage, as you'll need to handle repairs, tenant issues, and more.

REITs (Real Estate Investment Trusts)

A REIT is a way to invest in real estate without buying any property yourself. Instead, you put money into a fund that owns and manages buildings, like shopping malls, office buildings, or apartments. When these buildings make money (through rent or property sales), you earn a part of that income. REITs are a good option if you want to invest in real estate but don't want the responsibility of managing property.

Home Ownership

Buying your own home can also be an investment. While most people buy homes to live in, the value of homes can increase over time, giving you a profit if you sell it later. Home ownership doesn't provide monthly income, but it can help you build wealth as the home's value rises. Additionally, you save money on rent by owning instead of renting.

Each of these options—rental properties, REITs, and home ownership—has its benefits and challenges. Rental properties offer regular income, REITs give you access to real estate without the hassle, and home ownership can be a way to build wealth over time.

How Real Estate Can Be a Valuable Long-Term Investment

Real estate is considered a valuable long-term investment for several reasons. Here's why:

Appreciation

One of the main benefits of real estate is appreciation, which means the property value increases over time. For example, if you buy a house for $200,000 today, its value might grow to $300,000 in 10–20 years. This increase in value can give you a large profit if you sell the property in the future. Appreciation makes real estate a great option for long-term growth.

Regular Income from Rentals

If you own rental properties, you can earn a steady income every month from rent. This income can cover the property's expenses, like mortgage payments and maintenance, and still leave you with extra money. Over the years, rental income can build wealth and help cover other financial goals.

Diversification

Adding real estate to your investment portfolio diversifies your assets. This means you're not putting all your money into stocks or bonds. Real estate can grow separately from the stock market, helping you balance risk. If stocks go down, real estate might still do well, giving you a safer overall investment mix.

Tax Benefits

Real estate often comes with tax advantages. For instance, you can deduct certain costs, like mortgage interest, property taxes, and maintenance expenses, which lowers your tax bill. These benefits make real estate more affordable and profitable in the long run.

A Physical Asset

Unlike stocks or bonds, real estate is something you can see and use. You own the property, and it's there, physically, even if the market goes down temporarily. This makes real estate feel secure and reliable for many people.

Chapter 4

Getting Started with Your First Investment

Opening an Investment Account

Starting your first investment can feel exciting but also a bit overwhelming. The first step to getting started is opening an investment account, which is like a special bank account used just for investing. There are different types of accounts to consider, and each one serves a different purpose. Let's look at some common types and go through the steps to open one.

Types of Accounts to Consider

Brokerage Account

A brokerage account is the most common type of investment account. With a brokerage account, you can buy and sell investments like stocks, bonds, and mutual funds. This type of account is flexible, and you can put in or take out money whenever you want. A brokerage account is a good choice if you're investing for general goals, like saving for a big purchase or simply growing your money over time.

Retirement Accounts (401(k) and IRA)

Retirement accounts are special accounts designed to help you save for your future. The two main types are 401(k) and IRA (Individual Retirement Account).

401(k): If you have a job that offers a 401(k) plan, you can put a part of your paycheck into this account. Some employers even match a portion of what you contribute, adding extra money to your account. This type of account is tax-friendly, meaning you don't pay taxes on the money you put in until you take it out in retirement.

IRA: If your job doesn't offer a 401(k), you can open an IRA on your own. There are two types of IRAs: Traditional and Roth. With a Traditional IRA, you get a tax break on the money you put in now, but you'll pay taxes when you take it out in retirement. With a Roth IRA, you pay taxes now, but the money grows tax-free, meaning you won't pay taxes when you withdraw it in retirement.

Education Savings Accounts

If you're saving for education expenses, like college tuition, you can open a special account called a 529 plan. This account allows your money to grow tax-free if it's used for qualified education expenses. It's a good option if you have long-term goals related to education.

Custodial Accounts

Custodial accounts are opened by an adult for a child. Parents or guardians set up the account, and the money is held until the child reaches a certain age (usually 18 or 21). These accounts are a great way to start saving and investing for a child's future, whether for college or general needs.

Step-by-Step Guide to Opening Your First Investment Account

Now that you know the types of accounts, let's go through a simple step-by-step guide to open your first account.

Step 1: Decide on Your Goal

Before opening an account, think about what you're saving for. Are you planning for retirement, building a fund for college, or just growing your money? Your goal will help you decide which type of account to choose. If you're saving for retirement, an IRA or 401(k) is best. If it's for general investing, a brokerage account might be right for you.

Step 2: Choose a Brokerage or Financial Institution

To open an investment account, you need to choose a brokerage or financial institution. Many well-known companies, like Vanguard, Fidelity, Charles Schwab, and online platforms like Robinhood or E*TRADE, offer investment accounts. Look for one that has low fees, good customer service, and user-friendly online tools. You may also want to check if they offer educational resources if you're new to investing.

Step 3: Gather Your Information

When you open an account, you'll need to provide some basic information:
Personal Details: Your name, address, phone number, and Social Security Number (SSN).
Employment Information: Some brokerages ask for your job information.
Bank Details: To fund your account, you'll need to link it to a bank account. This allows you to transfer money in and out.
Make sure to have these details ready to speed up the process.

Step 4: Apply Online or In-Person

Most brokerages allow you to open an account online, which is the quickest way. Go to the website of your chosen brokerage and follow their instructions. They'll guide you through filling out forms and providing the necessary information. You can also visit a physical branch if they have one nearby and want to open the account in person.

Step 5: Choose Your Account Type and Funding Method

During the setup, select the type of account you want (like a brokerage or IRA). You'll also need to choose how you'll fund the account. Most brokerages offer several funding methods, including:
Bank Transfer: Link your bank account to transfer money directly.
Check: Some allow you to mail a check to deposit funds.
Direct Deposit: If it's a 401(k) or retirement account through your employer, you can set up direct deposits from your paycheck.
Decide how much money you want to start with. Many accounts don't have a minimum deposit, so you can start with a small amount if you'd like.

Step 6: Choose Your First Investments

Once your account is set up and funded, you're ready to invest! Most brokerages offer a range of choices, from stocks and bonds to mutual funds and ETFs. If you're not sure what to pick, many platforms have beginner-friendly tools to help you decide. You could also start by choosing a simple index fund or mutual fund to keep things easy.

Step 7: Review Your Account Regularly

After your account is up and running, make it a habit to review it regularly. Check on your investments, keep an eye on your goals, and make any changes if needed. Even small adjustments can help keep your investments on track over time.

How Much to Invest

Starting Small: How to Begin with What You Have

Many people think they need a lot of money to start investing, but this isn't true. You can begin with any amount, even if it's only a few dollars. Starting small lets you learn about investing without feeling pressured or worried about losing a lot. Small amounts also add up over time, and thanks to something called *compounding*, even small investments can grow surprisingly large as they earn returns.

For example, if you start with $20 and invest it each month, that small amount can grow into a larger sum over time. Many platforms, like investment apps, make it easy to start small, allowing you to buy pieces of stocks (called fractional shares) instead of a full share. So, don't worry if you can't invest much at first. Just putting a little bit away regularly is a great first step.

Understanding How Much You Should Invest Based on Your Goals and Income

When deciding how much to invest, it's important to look at two things: your financial goals and your income. Here's how to think about each of these:

Think About Your Goals

Your goals will affect how much you need to invest. If you have short-term goals, like saving for a vacation or a big purchase in the next couple of years, you may only need to invest a small amount regularly to reach them. For long-term goals, like retirement or buying a home, you'll likely need to invest more over time.

For example:

Short-Term Goals (1-2 years): You might need to invest small amounts monthly in a safer account, like a bond fund or high-yield savings account.
Medium-Term Goals (3-5 years): For goals in this range, investing a little more in a balanced fund of stocks and bonds can help you get a better return.
Long-Term Goals (10+ years): For goals that are far away, you may want to invest in stocks or mutual funds, which have more potential for growth.
Knowing your goals and their timelines helps you understand how much you should invest to reach them.

Consider Your Income

Your income affects how much you can afford to invest. A general rule some people use is to invest 10-15% of their income if possible. But if that feels too high, start with what you can manage comfortably. Even putting aside a small amount, like 5% of your income, can make a difference over time.
Let's say you earn $2,000 a month and aim to invest 5%. That would mean investing $100 each month. As you get more comfortable and possibly earn more, you can gradually increase this amount.

Balance Your Budget

Make sure that your investments fit within your budget. Cover all your necessary expenses first, like rent, bills, groceries, and emergency savings. The amount you invest should be something you can comfortably set aside without affecting your daily needs.

Adjust as You Go

As your goals or income change, you can adjust your investments. For example, if you get a raise, you might decide to increase the amount you invest. Or, if you're getting close to a goal, you may choose to put in a little extra to reach it sooner.

Building a Starter Portfolio

Creating a Simple, Diversified Portfolio

A starter portfolio is a collection of different investments that can help you grow your money while keeping your risk low. The goal is to have a mix of assets, so if one investment doesn't do well, others might still grow. This approach is called *diversification*, which simply means spreading your money across different types of investments to balance risk and growth.

When creating a starter portfolio, think about what you're saving for and how much risk you're comfortable taking. A simple, diversified portfolio usually includes a mix of stocks, bonds, and ETFs, which together give you a balance of safety and growth potential.

Chapter 5

Understanding Risk and Managing It

What is Investment Risk?

Investment risk is the chance that you might lose some or all of the money you invest. All investments come with some level of risk. For example, if you buy a stock, there's a chance its value could go down. Risk is something every investor faces, but learning about it helps you make smarter decisions and feel more prepared.

There are three main types of risks you should know about:

1. **Market Volatility**
    - Market volatility refers to how prices go up and down over time. Some days, the stock market is high, and other days, it's low. This movement is normal, but it can affect the value of your investments. If you invest in stocks or mutual funds, the prices of these investments will change daily, which can make them feel unpredictable.
    - For example, if you buy a stock at $10 and the next day it's $8, that's market volatility. However, if you're investing for the long term, you don't need to worry too much about daily ups and downs. Over time, markets tend to recover, and long-term investors can often see growth.
2. **Inflation**

- Inflation is when the cost of goods and services goes up over time. This means that your money won't buy as much in the future as it does today. For example, if inflation is 2%, something that costs $100 today might cost $102 next year.

- Inflation is a risk for your investments because if your money isn't growing faster than inflation, you're actually losing buying power. Some investments, like stocks, often grow faster than inflation, helping you keep up with rising costs. But safer investments, like savings accounts, might not grow fast enough to beat inflation, so it's important to find a balance.

3. Loss of Capital

- Loss of capital means losing the money you originally invested. This can happen if an investment doesn't perform well or if you sell it when the price is low. For example, if you invest $1,000 in a company that goes out of business, you could lose your entire investment.
- While this sounds scary, not all investments carry the same risk of losing money. Stocks and individual company investments are riskier, while bonds and certain funds are usually safer.

Understanding Risk Tolerance

Risk tolerance is the amount of risk you're comfortable taking with your investments. Everyone has a different tolerance, depending on their financial goals, age, income, and personality. Some people are fine with taking big risks if it means they might make a lot of money. Others prefer safer options that grow more slowly but have less chance of losing money. Knowing your risk tolerance helps you choose investments that feel right for you. Here's how to think about it:

Your Financial Situation

How much money you have, how much you earn, and how much you need to save affects your risk tolerance. If you have a steady income and some savings, you might feel comfortable taking more risk. But if your budget is tight, you may prefer safer investments.

For example, a young person who has many working years ahead might choose riskier investments like stocks because they have time to recover if the market goes down. On the other hand, someone closer to retirement might prefer safer options like bonds to protect their savings.

Your Investment Timeline

Your timeline, or how long you plan to keep your money invested, also affects your risk tolerance. If you're investing for a goal that's far away, like retirement in 20 or 30 years, you can handle more risk because you have time to wait out any market drops. But if your goal is closer, like buying a house in a few years, you might choose safer investments.

Long-term investors can often afford to take more risk because their investments have more time to grow and recover from losses. For short-term goals, you want stability, so lower-risk options like bonds are often better.

Your Comfort Level

Some people feel comfortable with the ups and downs of investing, while others feel nervous when their investments lose value. Your comfort level is a big part of risk tolerance. If you get stressed when investments drop, you may prefer safer options, even if it means slower growth.

It's important to pick investments that match your comfort level. This way, you're more likely to stay invested over time instead of selling too early because of worry.

Balancing Risk and Growth

To create a balanced investment strategy, you need to find a mix of investments that matches your risk tolerance and goals. This is why many investors use *diversification*, which means putting money into different types of investments. Here's how a balanced approach might look:

High-Risk Investments: Stocks are riskier but offer higher growth potential. If you can handle some ups and downs, putting part of your portfolio in stocks can help you grow your money faster.

Low-Risk Investments: Bonds and savings accounts are safer and more stable, but they grow slower. Having some money in these investments can give you a safety net.

Moderate-Risk Investments: Mutual funds and ETFs that hold a mix of stocks and bonds offer a balance between growth and safety, which can suit many investors well.

By combining different types of investments, you can build a portfolio that grows over time without taking on too much risk.

Strategies for Reducing Risk

Reducing risk is an important part of investing. Risk is the chance that you might lose money, but with some smart strategies, you can protect your investments and increase your chances of steady growth. Two key strategies for managing risk are *diversification* and focusing on *time in the market* rather than *timing the market.*

The Importance of Diversification

Diversification means spreading your money across different types of investments. This helps protect your portfolio from losing value if one area does poorly. Imagine you have a garden with many kinds of plants. If one type doesn't grow well, you still have other plants that are doing fine. Diversification in investing works the same way. By owning different types of investments, you create a "garden" that can survive different market conditions.

What Does Diversification Do?

Diversification helps reduce the risk of big losses. Different types of investments, or "asset classes," don't always move in the same direction. For example, when stocks go down, bonds might stay stable or even go up. This balance means that if one type of investment loses value, another type might still grow, helping to protect your overall portfolio.

Types of Asset Classes for Diversification

There are several main asset classes you can invest in:

1. Stocks: Shares in companies, which can grow a lot over time but can also go up and down.
2. Bonds: Loans to companies or governments that pay you interest and are usually safer than stocks.
3. Real Estate: Property or real estate funds that can increase in value and provide rental income.

4. Cash or Cash Equivalents: These include savings accounts and money market funds, which are very safe but don't grow as fast.

How to Diversify Within Each Asset Class

Not only can you diversify across different asset classes, but you can also diversify within each class. For example:

1. In stocks, you can choose shares from different industries, like technology, healthcare, and energy.
2. In bonds, you can pick bonds with different levels of safety, such as government bonds, which are very safe, and corporate bonds, which have slightly more risk.
3. In real estate, you could invest in both commercial properties (like offices) and residential properties (like homes).

By diversifying across and within asset classes, you create a portfolio that is less likely to lose a lot of value if one area has a bad year.

Why Diversification Helps Reduce Risk

Diversification reduces the risk of major losses because it spreads your investments across different areas. For example, if you only invested in technology stocks and the tech industry had a bad year, your entire portfolio might go down. But if you also owned bonds and real estate, those investments might stay stable or grow, balancing out the losses. Diversification is one of the easiest and most effective ways to protect your investments from sudden drops.

Time in the Market vs. Timing the Market

Another important strategy for reducing risk is focusing on *time in the market* rather than *timing the market.* Many people think that they need to buy investments at the "perfect" time to make money. They try to "time the market," which means guessing when prices will be low to buy and when they'll be high to sell. But predicting the market perfectly is extremely difficult, even for experts.

What is Time in the Market?

Time in the market means keeping your money invested for a long period, no matter what happens in the short term. When you invest for many years, you're more likely to see overall growth, even if there are temporary drops along the way. Over the long term, the stock market has historically gone up, so staying invested lets your money grow with the market.

Why Timing the Market is Risky

Timing the market can lead to mistakes because no one can predict exactly when prices will rise or fall. If you sell when prices drop out of fear, you might miss out on gains when prices go back up. This approach can also make you stressed about small ups and downs, leading to more emotional decisions.

How Time in the Market Reduces Risk

By focusing on time in the market, you give your investments time to recover from any drops. For example, if you buy a stock and it drops 10% next week, it might feel like a loss. But if you hold onto that stock for 10 or 20 years, the value could grow well beyond the original price. Long-term investing allows you to see the benefits of compounding growth, where your earnings also start to earn returns over time.

The Power of Compounding

Compounding is when the returns you make on your investments start earning returns too. For example, if you invest $1,000 and it grows by 10% in a year, you'll have $1,100. In the second year, that $1,100 grows by another 10%, giving you $1,210. Compounding becomes even more powerful over many years, turning small investments into larger amounts.

Examples of Time in the Market Success

One inspiring example of a Black female investor is **Teri Ijeoma**, a successful entrepreneur and stock market investor. Teri began her investing journey as a way to make extra money to support her goals and eventually leave her 9-to-5 job. Over time, she turned her part-time investment efforts into a full-time career and became an influential figure in the financial education space.

Teri's strategy focused on the long-term potential of the stock market. She started by learning the basics of investing and committing to a disciplined approach, even during periods of market uncertainty. By sticking to her plan and believing in the growth potential of her chosen investments, Teri was able to steadily grow her wealth over time. Her patience and dedication to staying invested, rather than reacting emotionally to market fluctuations, helped her achieve significant financial success.

Today, Teri shares her knowledge through her platform, **Trade and Travel**, teaching others—particularly women and people of color—how to build wealth through investing. Her story highlights how staying in the market and focusing on long-term goals can lead to incredible results, even for those who start with limited knowledge or resources. Her success is a testament to the power of patience and persistence in investing.

Combining Diversification and Time in the Market

The best way to manage risk is to use both diversification and time in the market together. By diversifying, you reduce the impact of any one investment losing value, and by staying invested for the long term, you give your portfolio the chance to grow steadily. Here's how these strategies work together:

A Diversified Portfolio

When you own a mix of stocks, bonds, real estate, and cash, you're better protected from losses. If stocks go down one year, your bonds or real estate investments might still do well, balancing your portfolio. This helps you avoid the worry of losing everything in one market dip.

Staying Invested Long-Term

By staying invested, you don't have to worry about timing the market perfectly. Even if you buy an investment during a high point, over many years, it has time to grow. This approach reduces the stress of daily ups and downs and gives your money the time it needs to benefit from compounding.

Using Dollar-Cost Averaging

What is Dollar-Cost Averaging?

Dollar-cost averaging is an investing strategy where you invest a set amount of money at regular intervals, like every week, month, or quarter. It means you don't have to worry about the ups and downs of the market because you're investing steadily over time. For example, if you decide to invest $100 every month, you stick to that amount whether the market is up or down.

The main idea behind dollar-cost averaging is that by investing a fixed amount regularly, you can reduce the impact of market changes. Since you're buying investments at different prices over time, you're not trying to guess the "perfect" time to invest. This approach makes it easier to stay calm, even if the market goes up and down.

How Dollar-Cost Averaging Works

Imagine you decide to invest $100 every month into a stock or mutual fund. Each month, the price of the stock might change, but you're still putting in the same amount. Sometimes, your $100 buys fewer shares if the price is high. Other times, it buys more shares if the price is low. Over time, the price averages out, which can help you pay a fair price without stressing about the best time to buy.

Here's an example:

Month 1: The stock price is $10. Your $100 buys 10 shares.

Month 2: The stock price drops to $8. Your $100 now buys 12.5 shares.

Month 3: The stock price rises to $12. Your $100 buys 8.33 shares.

In these three months, you invested a total of $300. You bought a total of 30.83 shares, making the average cost per share $9.73, which is lower than the highest price ($12) and not too far from the lowest price ($8).

By investing the same amount regularly, you don't have to worry about what the market is doing on a given day. You're buying when prices are high and low, which can help balance things out over time.

Benefits of Dollar-Cost Averaging

Easier to Start Investing

Dollar-cost averaging is a simple way to begin investing because it doesn't require a big lump sum. You can start with small amounts, like $50 or $100 a month. This makes it more affordable and easier to fit into your budget.

Reduces Emotional Decisions

One of the biggest challenges in investing is staying calm when the market drops. People often panic and sell when prices fall, only to miss out on gains when prices recover. Dollar-cost averaging helps you stick to a plan because you're investing consistently, no matter what happens in the market. By following this strategy, you're less likely to react emotionally to market changes.

Takes the Pressure Off Timing

Many people feel pressure to buy investments at the "perfect" time, but predicting the market is extremely hard, even for experts. Dollar-cost averaging removes this pressure. Instead of trying to time the market, you invest regularly, trusting that prices will average out over time. This way, you don't need to worry about whether the market is high or low on any given day.

Smooths Out Market Fluctuations

Dollar-cost averaging helps you deal with market fluctuations, or changes in prices. By investing regularly, you buy more shares when prices are low and fewer when prices are high. This approach balances out the cost, giving you an average price over time. As a result, you're less affected by sudden price changes, and your investment grows steadily.

Example of Dollar-Cost Averaging in Action

Let's say you decide to invest $1,200 over a year by putting in $100 every month. Here's how it might look if the stock price changes each month:
Month 1: Stock price is $10 → You buy 10 shares.
Month 2: Stock price is $8 → You buy 12.5 shares.
Month 3: Stock price is $6 → You buy 16.67 shares.
Month 4: Stock price is $9 → You buy 11.11 shares.
Month 5: Stock price is $11 → You buy 9.09 shares.
Month 6: Stock price is $10 → You buy 10 shares.
By the end of six months, you would have invested $600 and bought a total of about 69.37 shares. Your average cost per share is around $8.65, even though the price went as high as $11 and as low as $6. This average cost

shows how dollar-cost averaging smooths out the highs and lows, giving you a fair price over time.

Chapter 6

Investing For Retirement

Why Retirement Planning is Essential

Planning for retirement is about making sure you have enough money to live comfortably when you stop working. For most people, the income they make from working covers their needs, but this changes once they retire. That's why planning for retirement is so important. You want to have savings and investments that can support you in the years when you're no longer earning a regular paycheck.

The Importance of Starting Early

One of the most powerful tools in retirement planning is starting early. The sooner you start saving and investing, the more time your money has to grow. This is because of something called *compounding interest.*

What is Compounding Interest?

Compounding interest is when you earn interest on the money you've saved or invested, and then that interest also starts earning interest. It's like a snowball effect—your money keeps growing because both your original amount and the interest it makes are earning more interest.

How Compounding Works Over Time

Imagine you invest $1,000 with a 5% interest rate. In the first year, you earn $50 in interest, so now you have $1,050. In the second year, you earn interest on $1,050, so you get $52.50. This may not seem like a big difference at first, but over many years, the effect of compounding adds up. The more time you give your money to grow, the larger it can become.

Why Starting Early Makes a Big Difference

If you start saving for retirement at age 25, you have decades to let your money grow. Even small amounts can grow into a large retirement fund over time. For example, if you save $200 per month from age 25 to age 65 with a 5% return, you could end up with over $300,000. But if you start saving at 35 instead, you'd end up with less than half of that amount. The extra years make a big difference because compounding works best when it has time to build up.

The Cost of Waiting: Starting at 20 vs. Starting at 30

Saving for your future is like planting seeds in a garden. The earlier you plant, the more time your seeds have to grow into strong, fruitful trees. If you wait too long to plant, your trees won't have as much time to grow. This is the idea behind saving early for retirement. Let's look at how starting at age 20 compares to starting at age 30.

Imagine two people, Sarah and Lisa. Sarah begins saving $100 a month at age 20, while Lisa waits until she's 30 to start saving. Both plan to retire at age 60, and their savings earn a steady growth rate of 6% per year.

Sarah's Savings at Age 60

Sarah saves $100 every month from age 20 to 60. That's 40 years of saving, or $48,000 in total contributions. But thanks to something called compound interest, her savings grow far beyond what she puts in. Compound interest means Sarah earns money not just on the amount she saves but also on the interest her savings have already earned. By age 60, Sarah's total savings will have grown to about **$200,000.**

Lisa's Savings at Age 60

Lisa starts saving $100 a month at age 30 and continues until she's 60. That's 30 years of saving, or $36,000 in total contributions. Like Sarah, Lisa's savings also benefit from compound interest, but she has 10 fewer years for her money to grow. By the time Lisa reaches 60, her savings will have grown to about **$100,000.**

Comparing the Results

Even though Sarah only saved $12,000 more than Lisa, her total savings are **double** Lisa's because she started earlier. Those extra 10 years made a huge difference because her money had more time to grow.

The Bigger Picture

Now let's see what happens if Sarah and Lisa decide to save more each month. If they both save $200 a month instead of $100:

Sarah's total savings

Over 40 years, she contributes $96,000. With compound growth, her savings grow to around **$400,000** by age 60.

Lisa's total savings

Over 30 years, she contributes $72,000. With compound growth, her savings grow to about **$200,000** by age 60.

Again, Sarah has double the savings, even though she only saved $24,000 more than Lisa. This shows the power of starting early.

Why Waiting Costs More

If Lisa wanted to catch up with Sarah's savings by age 60, she would need to save around $200 a month starting at age 30 instead of $100. Waiting even longer would make the monthly amount she needs to save even higher.

The Key Takeaway

Starting early allows you to save smaller amounts while still reaching big goals. If you wait, you'll need to save much more each month to reach the same goal. Even small savings now can grow into something big over time, giving you a brighter and more secure future. The earlier you start, the easier it is to achieve your goals.

Risks of Relying Solely on Pensions or Social Security

Some people believe that pensions or Social Security will be enough to cover their retirement needs, but relying only on these sources can be risky. Here's why it's important to have your own savings and investments for retirement:

Understanding Pensions

A pension is a retirement plan offered by some employers. With a pension, the company puts money aside for you, and you receive a fixed amount of income in retirement. While pensions can be helpful, not all jobs offer them, and the amount you receive may not be enough to cover all your living expenses in retirement. In addition, some companies may change or reduce pension benefits over time.

Social Security

Social Security is a government program that provides retirement income based on how much you earned during your working years. While Social Security can help, it's often not enough to live on by itself. Social Security is meant to support basic needs, not to cover all expenses. If you have a mortgage, medical bills, or other costs, Social Security may not be enough.

The Reality of Rising Costs

As time goes by, the cost of living usually increases. Prices for food, healthcare, and housing tend to go up, which means that the income from pensions or Social Security may not keep up with your needs. Having your own retirement savings allows you to cover these additional costs.

The Uncertainty of Social Security

There is some uncertainty about the future of Social Security. While it's expected to be available, the exact amount people will receive could change. By saving on your own, you don't have to depend entirely on Social Security, giving you more control over your retirement income.

Having Control Over Your Retirement

By saving and investing for retirement, you have control over your financial future. You can decide how much you want to save, where you want to invest, and what kind of lifestyle you want in retirement. Relying solely on Social Security or a pension takes away some of this control because the amount you receive is decided by others.

How to Start Saving for Retirement

To avoid depending only on Social Security or a pension, it's smart to start saving and investing for retirement as soon as possible. Here are some ways to begin:

Open a Retirement Account

In the United States, there are special accounts designed for retirement, like a 401(k) or an IRA. These accounts have tax benefits, making it easier to save and grow your money over time.

Use a 401(k) Plan

A 401(k) is an employer-sponsored retirement plan. If your job offers a 401(k), it's a good idea to take advantage of it. Many employers match a part of what you put in, so if you contribute $1,000, your employer might add another $500. This is like free money that grows over time.

Consider an IRA

If your employer doesn't offer a 401(k) or you want to save more, you can open an IRA (Individual Retirement Account). There are two main types: Traditional and Roth. In a Traditional IRA, you don't pay taxes on the money you put in until you take it out. In a Roth IRA, you pay taxes now, but your withdrawals are tax-free in retirement. Both types help your savings grow over time.

Automate Your Savings

Setting up automatic contributions is a simple way to save consistently. By putting a set amount into your retirement account each month, you don't have to remember to save—it happens automatically. This also helps build discipline and keeps you on track with your goals.

Increase Contributions Over Time

If you can, try to increase the amount you're saving each year, especially if you get a raise. Even a small increase can make a big difference over many years. Starting with a manageable amount and gradually increasing it can help you build a strong retirement fund.

Benefits of Having Your Own Retirement Savings

Security

Having your own retirement savings gives you security and peace of mind. You don't have to worry about changes in Social Security or pensions because you have a separate source of income for retirement.

Flexibility

With your own retirement savings, you have more options. You can choose when you want to retire and what kind of lifestyle you want. You might even be able to retire early if you save enough.

Leaving a Legacy

If you save and invest wisely, you may have money left over for your family or causes you care about. This allows you to support loved ones or make a positive impact, even after you're gone.

Retirement Accounts

When saving for retirement, there are special accounts designed to help you grow your money with extra benefits. These accounts are called retirement accounts, and the main ones in the U.S. are 401(k) plans, Traditional IRAs, and Roth IRAs. Each type has its own rules, benefits, and ways to help you save more effectively for retirement.

1. 401(k) Plans

A 401(k) is a retirement savings plan offered by many employers in the U.S. If your job offers a 401(k), it's a great place to start saving for retirement because it has unique benefits.

How a 401(k) Works:

With a 401(k), you choose how much money you want to save each pay period. This amount is automatically taken out of your paycheck and put into your 401(k) account before taxes are taken out, which means you're saving money without having to think about it each month.

Tax Advantages:

The money you put into a 401(k) isn't taxed until you take it out in retirement. This is called "tax-deferred" growth. Since your money is growing tax-free, you have more to invest, which helps your savings grow faster. You'll pay taxes on the money only when you withdraw it in retirement.

Investment Options:

Inside your 401(k), you can usually choose from a variety of investment options like stocks, bonds, and mutual funds. Your employer might even provide tools to help you pick the investments that fit your retirement goals.

2. Traditional IRAs

If your job doesn't offer a 401(k), or if you want to save even more, you can open an Individual Retirement Account (IRA). A Traditional IRA is a retirement account you open on your own, and it has some similarities to a 401(k).

How a Traditional IRA Works:

With a Traditional IRA, you contribute money that can often be deducted from your taxable income, lowering your tax bill now. The money grows tax-free until you take it out in retirement, similar to a 401(k).

Contribution Limits:

There are limits on how much you can put into an IRA each year. For 2023, for example, the contribution limit is $6,500 if you're under age 50, or $7,500 if you're 50 or older. These limits are adjusted from time to time, so it's good to check the current amount each year.

3. Roth IRAs

A Roth IRA is another type of retirement account you open on your own, but it has a unique tax benefit.

How a Roth IRA Works:

With a Roth IRA, you put in money that has already been taxed, meaning you don't get an immediate tax break like with a 401(k) or Traditional IRA. However, when you take the money out in retirement, you won't owe any taxes on it. Both the money you put in and any gains are tax-free when withdrawn.

Tax-Free Withdrawals:

The main advantage of a Roth IRA is that your withdrawals in retirement are completely tax-free. This can be a huge benefit if you expect to be in a higher tax bracket when you retire or if you want to keep more of your retirement income for yourself.

Eligibility Limits:

Not everyone can contribute to a Roth IRA. If your income is above a certain level, you may not be able to add to a Roth IRA, so it's important to check the income limits each year.

How to Maximize Employer-Matching Contributions and Tax Benefits

To get the most out of your retirement accounts, there are strategies you can use. Here's how to make the most of employer matching and tax benefits:

Employer-Matching Contributions

Many companies that offer a 401(k) plan also provide an *employer match*. This means they contribute a certain amount to your 401(k) based on how much you contribute. It's like free money that helps your retirement savings grow faster.

How Employer Matching Works:

Let's say your employer matches 50% of what you contribute, up to a certain percentage of your salary. For example, if you contribute 6% of your salary to your 401(k), they'll add an extra 3%. This match is essentially free money that boosts your savings.

Make Sure to Contribute Enough:

To get the full benefit of employer matching, try to contribute enough to reach the maximum match. For example, if your employer matches up to 6%, make sure you're putting in at least 6% of your salary. Otherwise, you're leaving free money on the table.

Automatic Contribution Increases:

Some 401(k) plans allow you to set up automatic increases, meaning your contributions go up a little each year. This is a helpful way to save more over time without feeling a big difference in your paycheck.

Take Advantage of Tax Benefits

The tax benefits of retirement accounts help your money grow faster because you're keeping more of it working for you.

401(k) and Traditional IRA Tax Deferral:

When you contribute to a 401(k) or Traditional IRA, you're lowering your taxable income. This means you pay less in taxes now. Since the money grows tax-free until you take it out, you have more to invest over the years, which can lead to larger savings in retirement.

Roth IRA Tax-Free Withdrawals:

With a Roth IRA, you're paying taxes upfront but won't owe any taxes when you withdraw in retirement. This is especially beneficial if you think taxes will be higher in the future. By paying taxes now, you lock in your tax rate and can enjoy tax-free income later.

Balancing Traditional and Roth Accounts:

If you're not sure which option is best, you can use a combination of both. For example, you could contribute to a 401(k) at work and also open a Roth IRA. This gives you tax savings now and tax-free withdrawals in retirement, which provides flexibility when you retire.

Max Out Contributions When Possible

The government sets limits on how much you can contribute to retirement accounts each year. If you're able to, maxing out these contributions can give your savings a big boost.

401(k) Contribution Limits:

For 2023, you can contribute up to $22,500 to a 401(k) if you're under 50, or $30,000 if you're 50 or older. If you can afford to contribute the maximum, you'll build your savings faster and take full advantage of the tax benefits.

IRA Contribution Limits:

As mentioned, for IRAs, the 2023 limit is $6,500, or $7,500 if you're over 50. Maxing out your IRA contributions each year can help you reach your retirement goals sooner.

Keep Track of Fees and Investment Choices

When using retirement accounts, pay attention to fees and investment options. High fees can eat into your returns, so look for low-cost funds within your 401(k) or IRA.

Choosing Low-Fee Investments:

Many retirement accounts offer mutual funds or index funds with low fees. Choosing these options can save you money over time and help your retirement savings grow.

Regularly Review and Adjust:

It's a good idea to check your retirement accounts once or twice a year to make sure your investments match your goals. If you need to make changes, such as adjusting the mix of stocks and bonds, you can do that within your retirement accounts.

Creating a Retirement Investment Strategy

A retirement investment strategy is a plan that helps you grow your money over time so that you'll have enough for a comfortable life when you stop working. Creating this plan involves choosing the right mix of investments and adjusting them as you get closer to retirement. Here, we'll explore how to allocate your investments for long-term growth and how to adjust your strategy as you age.

Allocating Investments for Long-Term Growth

When investing for retirement, your goal is to grow your money over many years. To do this, you need to decide how to divide, or allocate, your money among different types of investments. Each type has its own level of risk and potential return.

Stocks for Growth

Stocks are shares of companies and have the highest growth potential. Over time, stocks have generally provided the biggest returns, making them essential for retirement investments. However, stocks are also more volatile, which means their prices can go up and down.

When you're young and have many years until retirement, it's generally safe to have a large portion of your retirement fund in stocks. This is because you have time to wait for the value of stocks to recover if they drop. Many financial experts suggest that young investors keep around 70%–90% of their retirement money in stocks.

Bonds for Stability

Bonds are loans to companies or governments. They are safer than stocks and provide steady returns through interest payments. Bonds help balance out the risk of stocks, making your portfolio more stable.

A common approach is to hold 10%–30% of your retirement fund in bonds when you're young. As you get older, you'll increase this percentage because bonds provide a safer way to protect your money as retirement gets closer.

Cash and Cash Equivalents for Security

Cash equivalents are very safe, low-risk options like money market funds or short-term bonds. These don't grow much, but they're reliable and easy to access. Having some cash in your retirement portfolio gives you flexibility and a safety cushion if you need quick access to money.

Most people don't need to hold much cash when they're young since it doesn't grow much. As you get closer to retirement, you'll gradually increase your cash holdings to keep your retirement fund stable.

Real Estate for Additional Growth

Real estate, such as investing in property or Real Estate Investment Trusts (REITs), can be another way to grow your retirement fund. Real estate values tend to go up over time, and REITs allow you to invest in real estate without having to buy property directly.

While not everyone includes real estate in their retirement plan, it can be a good option for adding diversity to your investments. Some people put around 5%–15% of their retirement savings in real estate.

Example of a Young Investor's Retirement Portfolio

For someone in their 20s or 30s, a typical retirement portfolio might look like this:

80% in Stocks: For growth.

15% in Bonds: For stability.

5% in Cash Equivalents: For flexibility.

This mix focuses on growth while adding some stability, which helps you build a solid retirement fund over time.

Adjusting Your Strategy as You Age

As you get closer to retirement, you'll want to adjust your investment strategy. The goal is to reduce risk and protect the savings you've built. Here's how to shift your investments as you age:

In Your 40s: Preparing for Changes

In your 40s, you still have plenty of time for your investments to grow, but it's a good idea to start adding more bonds for stability. At this stage, you might change your allocation to about 70% in stocks, 25% in bonds, and 5% in cash equivalents.

This mix keeps your portfolio growing while also starting to lower the risk. Adding bonds provides more stability, which can help protect your savings if the stock market drops.

In Your 50s: Reducing Risk

In your 50s, retirement is getting closer, so reducing risk becomes more important. During this decade, you might adjust your portfolio to around 60% in stocks, 30% in bonds, and 10% in cash equivalents.

Having more bonds and cash makes your portfolio steadier, as these types of investments don't fluctuate as much as stocks. Keeping a smaller percentage in stocks still allows for growth but with less risk.

In Your 60s: Focusing on Stability

In your 60s, many people start to think about retiring. At this point, you'll want to protect the money you've built by moving more of it into bonds and cash. A common strategy is to hold about 40% in stocks, 40% in bonds, and 20% in cash equivalents.

This mix is much safer than a stock-heavy portfolio. Bonds and cash give you steady returns and easy access to money, which is useful as you start using your retirement savings.

After Retirement: Keeping It Safe

Once you're retired, the goal is to make sure your money lasts. You'll probably keep only a small portion in stocks, like 20%–30%, to keep up with inflation. The rest can go into bonds and cash for safety.

This setup protects your retirement fund and ensures that you have enough money to cover your living expenses for many years.

Rebalancing Your Portfolio Regularly

As you adjust your portfolio with age, it's also important to rebalance it regularly. Rebalancing means checking your investments once a year or so to make sure they're still in line with your plan. Over time, some investments may grow faster than others, changing your allocation. For example, if your stocks grow a lot one year, they may end up making up a larger percentage of your portfolio than you planned. Rebalancing helps you get back to your target allocation by buying or selling investments as needed.

Benefits of Adjusting Your Retirement Strategy

Managing Risk

By shifting from stocks to bonds and cash as you age, you manage risk and protect your savings. This keeps your retirement fund safer, especially as you approach the time when you'll need to start using it.

Ensuring Steady Income

Bonds and cash provide steady returns, which can serve as income during retirement. This gives you financial security without having to worry about market ups and downs affecting your money.

Avoiding Panic Selling

With a safer portfolio as you age, you're less likely to panic and sell when markets drop. Bonds and cash help keep your savings stable, so you're not forced to sell stocks at a low price if the market dips.

Making Your Money Last

By adjusting your portfolio, you make sure your money lasts for the rest of your life. A safe mix of bonds and cash, with a small amount of stocks, allows you to cover expenses and keep some growth for the future.

Chapter 7

Real Estate Investing For Beginners

Why Real Estate is a Powerful Investment

Real estate is a popular investment choice because it provides multiple ways to build wealth. When you invest in real estate, you are buying property—like houses, apartments, or commercial buildings—that can increase in value over time and generate income. Here's how real estate can help you build wealth through appreciation, rental income, and tax benefits.

How Real Estate Builds Wealth

Appreciation

Appreciation means that the value of your property goes up over time. For example, if you buy a house for $200,000 and it's worth $250,000 five years later, it has appreciated by $50,000. Real estate generally appreciates over time because as more people need places to live, work, and shop, property becomes more valuable.

Many people who invest in real estate aim to hold onto their property for a long time, letting it appreciate so they can sell it later at a higher price. This long-term growth can be a great way to build wealth.

Rental Income

Another way to make money from real estate is through rental income. If you buy a property and rent it out, tenants pay you rent each month. This rent can provide a steady income, which can cover the property's mortgage, maintenance, and other costs, with some left over as profit.

For example, if you buy a rental home and your tenants pay $1,500 per month, that's $18,000 a year in rental income. As long as your expenses are lower than this amount, you're making a profit. This income can also grow over time, as you can increase rent to match the cost of living or property improvements.

Tax Benefits

Real estate offers some unique tax benefits that can save you money. For instance, you can deduct certain expenses related to the property, such as mortgage interest, property taxes, repairs, and maintenance, from your taxable income. These deductions lower the amount of taxes you owe, which helps you keep more of your rental income.

Additionally, real estate investors can use a tax benefit called depreciation, which lets you deduct the cost of the property over time, even if it's going up in value. This can provide a big tax break, especially for rental property owners.

Pros and Cons of Investing in Real Estate Compared to Stocks and Bonds

Real estate has its own advantages and disadvantages when compared to other types of investments like stocks and bonds. Here's a look at some of the pros and cons to help you decide if it's right for you.

Pros of Investing in Real Estate

Tangible Asset

Real estate is a physical, tangible asset—you can see and use it. Unlike stocks or bonds, which are just numbers on a screen, real estate is something you own in the real world. This makes it feel more secure to many people.

Steady Income

With rental properties, you can earn a steady monthly income from tenants. This income can help you pay off the mortgage and other expenses, providing extra cash each month. Rental income is often more predictable than the returns on stocks, making it a good option if you want regular cash flow.

Long-Term Appreciation

Real estate values tend to rise over time, which makes it a good choice for long-term investors. Property prices often keep up with or exceed inflation, which means your investment can grow in value over the years.

Tax Advantages

As mentioned, real estate provides tax benefits that aren't available with other types of investments. Deductions for mortgage interest, property taxes, and depreciation can help you save on taxes, which is a huge advantage if you own rental properties.

Ability to Leverage

Leverage means using borrowed money to increase the potential return on your investment. In real estate, you can take out a mortgage to buy a property, meaning you don't have to pay the full price upfront. For example, with a 20% down payment on a $200,000 property, you only need $40,000. If the property value goes up, you benefit from the increase on the entire $200,000, not just the $40,000 you invested.

Cons of Investing in Real Estate

Requires Large Initial Investment

Real estate usually requires a big upfront payment, such as a down payment and closing costs. This can make it harder to get started compared to stocks and bonds, which you can buy with small amounts of money.

Ongoing Expenses and Maintenance

Owning property means you're responsible for repairs, maintenance, and other costs like property taxes and insurance. If something breaks, you have to pay to fix it, which can reduce your profit. This makes real estate more hands-on and time-consuming than other investments.

Liquidity Issues

Real estate is not a liquid asset, meaning it can take time to sell and turn into cash. If you need money quickly, it's harder to sell a house or property than it is to sell stocks or bonds. This lack of liquidity can be a downside if you need access to your investment funds.

Market Fluctuations

Just like stocks, real estate can go through ups and downs. Property values don't always rise; they can drop in certain situations, like during economic downturns. If you need to sell during a market slump, you could lose money on the property.

Risk of Bad Tenants

If you rent out your property, there's always a risk of getting tenants who don't pay rent on time or who damage the property. Dealing with these issues can be stressful and may require legal action, which adds to the cost and effort of owning rental property.

Real Estate vs. Stocks and Bonds

Real estate, stocks, and bonds each have unique advantages and challenges. Here's a quick comparison:

Growth Potential

Stocks generally have a high growth potential, but real estate can also grow well over time, especially with appreciation and rental income. Bonds offer lower but steady returns.

Income

Real estate and bonds can provide steady income—rental income from property and interest from bonds. Stocks may pay dividends, but they are not as reliable as rental income.

Risk Level

Real estate has moderate risk since it depends on the property market and tenant stability. Stocks are higher risk due to market volatility, while bonds are usually safer.

Liquidity

Stocks and bonds are liquid, meaning you can sell them quickly if needed. Real estate is not as liquid, as selling property can take time.

Management Effort

Real estate requires more hands-on management, especially with rental properties. Stocks and bonds require minimal management, especially if you invest in mutual funds or ETFs.

Is Real Estate Right for You?

Whether real estate is the right investment for you depends on your goals, finances, and willingness to manage property. Real estate can be a powerful way to build wealth, especially if you're interested in a long-term investment that provides income, tax benefits, and appreciation. However, it's more hands-on than other investments, and you'll need to be prepared for the upfront costs, maintenance, and the time it takes to manage or sell property.

Types of Real Estate Investments

Investing in real estate offers different ways to make money and reach your financial goals. Each type of real estate investment works differently and has its own benefits and challenges. Here, we'll explore four main types: rental properties, commercial real estate, Real Estate Investment Trusts (REITs), and flipping homes. We'll also discuss how to decide which type suits your goals.

Rental Properties

Rental properties are one of the most common types of real estate investments. With a rental property, you buy a house, apartment, or building and rent it out to tenants who pay you rent each month. Rental income can cover your property expenses and give you a steady cash flow, which can make it a great option for long-term income.

How Rental Properties Work:

After buying a property, you can rent it out to tenants who pay monthly rent. This rent becomes your income. Ideally, the rent covers your mortgage (if you have one), property taxes, repairs, and other costs, with some money left over as profit.

Over time, the property may also appreciate, meaning it increases in value. When you sell it later, you could make additional profit from this appreciation.

Pros:

Steady monthly income.

Property appreciates over time.

Tax benefits, like deductions for mortgage interest and property expenses.

Cons:

Requires ongoing maintenance.

Potential issues with tenants (e.g., late payments or property damage).

High upfront costs, like a down payment and repairs.

Rental properties can be a good choice if you want regular income and are prepared to manage property and tenants. They're a long-term investment, so they work well for those looking to build wealth slowly.

Commercial Real Estate

Commercial real estate involves properties used for businesses, such as office buildings, shopping centers, warehouses, and hotels. Businesses rent these spaces to operate their stores, offices, or facilities.

How Commercial Real Estate Works:

You buy a property and rent it to companies or businesses. The lease terms are usually longer than with residential properties, often ranging from 3 to 10 years. This provides a steady and reliable income stream. Commercial tenants usually take care of maintenance and property expenses, making it less hands-on than residential rentals.

Pros:

Higher rental income than residential properties.

Long-term leases provide stable cash flow.

Businesses often take care of maintenance and utilities.

Cons:

More expensive to buy than residential properties.

Longer vacancy periods if a tenant leaves.

Sensitive to economic changes—businesses may downsize or close, affecting demand.

Commercial real estate is suitable for investors who can handle the higher cost and are looking for more income. It's often best for experienced investors, as it requires a strong understanding of the business market and involves bigger financial risks.

Real Estate Investment Trusts (REITs)

REITs, or Real Estate Investment Trusts, offer a way to invest in real estate without directly buying property. A REIT is a company that owns, operates, or finances real estate, such as shopping malls, apartment buildings, or office spaces. By buying shares of a REIT, you become a part-owner of that company's properties.

How REITs Work:

When you buy shares in a REIT, you're investing in a collection of properties managed by the REIT. The REIT earns money from renting out these properties and may also buy and sell properties for profit. REITs pay dividends to shareholders, which is a portion of the rental income and profits.

REITs are bought and sold like stocks on the stock market, so they're easy to buy and sell. They also have different types, including equity REITs (own properties), mortgage REITs (lend money for property purchases), and hybrid REITs (combine both owning and lending).

Pros:

Easy to buy and sell like stocks.

Provides a way to invest in real estate without buying property.

Steady income from dividends.

Cons:

Dividends are taxed as regular income, which can be higher than capital gains tax.

REITs depend on market conditions, so their prices can go up and down.

Less control over the specific properties owned by the REIT.

REITs are ideal for beginners or those who want to invest in real estate without managing property. They offer income through dividends, making them a good option for people looking for liquidity, or easy access to cash, without the hassle of property ownership.

Flipping Homes

Flipping homes is when you buy a property, improve it, and then sell it for a profit. This strategy focuses on buying low, renovating to add value, and selling high. House flipping is a short-term investment compared to renting or commercial real estate, but it requires a lot of work and knowledge.

How Flipping Homes Works:

You buy a property that needs repairs or upgrades, then fix it up to increase its market value. Once the property is improved, you sell it for more than what you paid, aiming to make a profit. The key is to choose properties in good locations where demand is high, and to keep renovation costs low so you can maximize profits.

Pros:

Quick profit, usually within a few months to a year.
No need to deal with long-term tenants.
Potential for high returns if done correctly.

Cons:

High costs for purchase and renovations.
Time-consuming and requires experience in real estate and renovations.
Financial risk if the property doesn't sell or the market drops.
Flipping homes can be profitable if you have real estate knowledge and are prepared for the work and risk. It's a good choice if you want short-term returns, but it's best for people with experience in property renovation or those working with a trusted team.

Choosing the Right Type of Real Estate Investment for Your Goals

When deciding which type of real estate investment suits you, think about your financial goals, available time, and experience level. Here's how to determine which option might be the best fit:

If You Want Steady Income

Best Option: Rental properties or REITs.

Rental properties give you monthly income from tenants, while REITs provide dividends without the hands-on work of managing property. If you're looking for income with less focus on appreciation, both options are good choices.

If You Have a Large Budget and Want Higher Returns

Best Option: Commercial real estate.

Commercial properties can offer higher rental income, especially if you can afford the upfront cost. However, this is best for experienced investors who are comfortable with the risks and costs involved.

If You Want to Invest in Real Estate Without Managing Property

Best Option: REITs.

REITs allow you to invest in real estate without buying property or managing tenants. They're easy to buy and sell, making them a good choice if you prefer a simpler way to earn from real estate.

If You Want Quick Returns and Enjoy Renovation

Best Option: Flipping homes.

Flipping homes can bring fast profits, but it requires knowledge and work. It's best if you're experienced in real estate or have the skills to manage property renovations. Flipping can be profitable in the short term but comes with high financial risks.

If You Want Long-Term Growth and Don't Mind Managing Property

Best Option: Rental properties.

Rental properties provide steady income and grow in value over time. This is a good option for investors who want long-term wealth and are comfortable with the responsibilities of property management.

Getting Started in Real Estate

Starting in real estate investing can be a great way to build wealth, whether you're buying your first rental property or investing in Real Estate Investment Trusts (REITs). Each option has its own steps and things to consider. Here's a simple guide to help you get started, including how to buy a rental property or invest in REITs, and how to research markets, calculate ROI, and manage your investment.

Steps to Purchasing Your First Rental Property

Buying a rental property is a big decision that requires planning and research. Here are the main steps to get you started:

Save for a Down Payment and Other Costs

Most rental properties need a down payment, typically around 20% of the property's price. For example, if you're buying a $200,000 property, you'll need at least $40,000 for the down payment. You'll also need money for closing costs, repairs, and any updates you want to make before renting it out.

Check Your Finances and Get Pre-Approved for a Loan

Make sure your finances are in order before applying for a loan. This means checking your credit score, paying off any high-interest debt, and saving up for unexpected expenses. Once you're ready, get pre-approved for a mortgage, which tells you how much you can borrow and shows sellers you're a serious buyer.

Research the Market

Location is key in real estate. Look for areas where people want to live, with good schools, public transportation, and job opportunities. Also, compare property prices and rental rates in the area. If properties are affordable and rent prices are high, you're more likely to earn a profit.

Find a Property That Fits Your Budget

Look for properties that are priced within your budget and have rental potential. Some buyers work with a real estate agent who specializes in rental properties to find a good match. You might start with a single-family home, duplex, or condo.

Calculate the Expected ROI (Return on Investment)

Before buying, calculate the property's potential ROI to see if it's worth the investment. This means estimating how much rental income you'll earn versus your expenses, such as mortgage payments, taxes, maintenance, and property management fees.

Purchase and Prepare the Property

Once you buy the property, get it ready for tenants. This may involve cleaning, repairs, or upgrades. Make sure it meets local safety standards and is in good condition. Then, set your rental price based on what similar properties are charging in the area.

Find Tenants and Start Managing the Property

Advertise your property to find tenants. You can use online rental platforms or work with a property manager if you don't want to handle this yourself. Once tenants move in, you'll manage the property, which includes collecting rent, handling maintenance, and addressing any issues.

Steps to Investing in REITs

If you want to invest in real estate without buying property, REITs offer a simpler option. REITs are companies that own or manage properties, and by buying shares, you can earn income from these properties without owning them directly.

Choose a Brokerage Account

To buy REITs, you'll need a brokerage account. There are many online platforms like Fidelity, Vanguard, or E*TRADE where you can open an account. Once you set it up, you can buy and sell REITs like stocks.

Research REITs

There are different types of REITs, including those that focus on residential properties, commercial buildings, or even healthcare facilities. Look at the REIT's past performance, dividend payouts (which is the income you earn), and the types of properties it owns. Reading the REIT's annual report can give you a better idea of how it manages properties and makes money.

Buy REIT Shares

Once you've chosen a REIT, buy shares through your brokerage account. You can start with a small amount, making it an easy way to get into real estate investing without needing a large upfront payment.

Monitor and Reinvest

REITs pay dividends, which is money you receive based on the profits the REIT makes from its properties. You can take this money as income or reinvest it to buy more shares, which can help grow your investment over time.

Researching Markets and Calculating ROI

Whether buying a rental property or investing in REITs, researching the market and calculating ROI are crucial steps to ensure a profitable investment.

Researching Markets

The real estate market can vary widely depending on the location. To find a good market:

Look for Growing Areas: Areas with job growth, good schools, and new businesses tend to attract more renters.

Check Local Rental Demand: High rental demand means you're more likely to find tenants quickly. You can check this by looking at rental vacancy rates, which show how many rental properties are empty.

Compare Prices and Rents: Compare home prices with rental rates. If rental rates are high compared to home prices, it may be easier to make a profit.

Calculating ROI (Return on Investment)

ROI tells you how much money you're making compared to what you invested. For a rental property, it's calculated as follows:

$ROI=(\text{Annual Rental Income}-\text{Annual Expenses}/\text{Total Investment}) \times 100$

Example Calculation:

- Annual Rental Income: $18,000
- Annual Expenses (mortgage, repairs, etc.):

$12,000

- Net Income:

$\text{Net Income}=\text{Annual Rental Income}-\text{Annual Expenses}$

=18,000−12,000= 6,000\text {Net Income} = \text {Annual Rental Income} - \text {Annual Expenses} = 18,000 - 12,000 = 6,000

$\text{Net Income}=\text{Annual Rental Income}-$
$\text{Annual Expenses}=18{,}000-12{,}000=6{,}000$

- Total Investment: $60,000

Using the formula:

$ROI = (6000/60{,}000) \times 100$

$ROI = 0.10 \times 100 = 10\%$

Result:

A 10% ROI means that you're earning a 10% return on your investment annually. This is generally considered good, but what qualifies as a "good" ROI can vary based on factors like property type, location, and individual financial goals.

Managing Real Estate Investments

After buying a property or REITs, managing your investment properly is essential for continued success.

Managing a Rental Property

Maintenance and Repairs: Keep the property in good condition by handling repairs quickly. This keeps tenants happy and protects the property's value.
Collecting Rent: Set up a reliable rent collection method, like online payments, to make sure you receive rent on time.

Dealing with Tenants: Respond promptly to tenant issues and treat them fairly. Good tenant relationships reduce the chances of tenant turnover, which helps maintain steady income.

If you prefer not to manage the property yourself, consider hiring a property management company. They handle everything from finding tenants to dealing with maintenance, though they typically charge a fee (usually around 10% of the monthly rent).

Managing REITs

REITs require less active management since you're investing through a brokerage account. To manage REIT investments:

Monitor Performance: Check the REIT's performance and dividends over time. If the REIT is performing well and paying regular dividends, you may want to keep your shares.

Reinvest Dividends: Many brokerage accounts offer a reinvestment option, allowing you to use dividends to buy more shares automatically.

Stay Updated: Follow news related to the real estate market and the specific types of properties your REIT owns. Economic changes can affect certain types of properties more than others, so staying informed can help you make better decisions.

Chapter 8

Investing In The Stock Market

How the Stock Market Works

The stock market is one of the most popular ways to invest and grow wealth over time. It's a place where you can buy and sell ownership shares, called "stocks," of different companies. Understanding how the stock market works can help you make smart choices as you start investing. These are the two largest stock exchanges in the United States. The New York Stock Exchange (NYSE) is known for its traditional trading floor and listing of large, established companies, while the National Association of Securities Dealers Automated Quotations (NASDAQ) is more technology-driven, hosting many tech and growth-oriented companies.

How the Stock Market Works

The stock market is a marketplace where people buy and sell shares of publicly traded companies. A "share" represents a tiny piece of ownership in a company. For example, if you buy a share of Apple, you own a small part of that company.

Companies sell shares on the stock market to raise money for various purposes, like developing new products or expanding their business. When you buy a share, you're investing in the company, hoping its value will increase over time so that you can make a profit by selling it at a higher price.

Overview of Stock Exchanges

To make it easy for people to buy and sell stocks, companies list their shares on stock exchanges. Stock exchanges are like big marketplaces that connect buyers and sellers. Two of the most well-known stock exchanges in the United States are the New York Stock Exchange (NYSE) and the NASDAQ.

New York Stock Exchange (NYSE)

The NYSE is the largest stock exchange in the world, and it has been around for over 200 years. It's located in New York City on Wall Street and is often thought of as the heart of the financial world. Companies listed on the NYSE are usually large, well-established companies, often referred to as "blue-chip" companies. Examples include Coca-Cola, Johnson & Johnson, and Walmart.

The NYSE operates during regular trading hours, from 9:30 AM to 4:00 PM Eastern Time on weekdays. During these hours, buyers and sellers can trade stocks on the exchange.

NASDAQ

The NASDAQ is another major stock exchange, but it operates differently from the NYSE. The NASDAQ is an electronic exchange, meaning all trades happen online through a network of computers. The NASDAQ is known for listing technology and growth companies, such as Apple, Microsoft, and Tesla.

Like the NYSE, the NASDAQ is open from 9:30 AM to 4:00 PM Eastern Time on weekdays. The NASDAQ's electronic system allows it to operate quickly and efficiently, which is important for companies in the fast-moving tech industry.

Both the NYSE and NASDAQ provide a platform for people to buy and sell stocks. While each exchange has its differences, they both play a key role in connecting investors with companies.

How Stock Prices Fluctuate Based on Supply and Demand

One of the most important things to understand about the stock market is how stock prices change. Stock prices fluctuate, or go up and down, based on supply and demand. Supply and demand are two forces that affect how much people are willing to pay for a stock.

What is Supply?

In the stock market, supply refers to the number of shares available for sale. When more people want to sell a stock than buy it, there is a high supply, which usually pushes the price down. This is because sellers might lower their price to attract buyers.

What is Demand?

Demand is the opposite of supply—it's how many people want to buy a stock. If more people want to buy a stock than sell it, demand is high. This often drives the price up, as buyers are willing to pay more to own the stock. When supply and demand are balanced, the stock price remains steady. However, if demand increases and more people want to buy, the price will rise. If demand drops and more people want to sell, the price will fall. Here's a simple example:

High Demand: If a lot of people believe a company is doing well, they may all want to buy its stock. As more people try to buy, the price goes up.

High Supply: If investors think a company is struggling, they may try to sell its stock. As more people sell, the price goes down.

Factors That Affect Supply and Demand

Several factors influence the supply and demand for a stock, which causes the price to fluctuate. Here are some key factors:

Company Performance

When a company performs well— earning high profits or launching successful products—its stock usually becomes more attractive to investors. High performance often leads to high demand, which increases the stock price. On the other hand, if a company reports losses or faces problems, demand may drop, and the stock price may fall.

Economic Conditions

The overall economy can impact stock prices. For example, in a strong economy with low unemployment and rising incomes, people feel more confident about investing, which can increase demand for stocks. In a weak economy or during a recession, people may be less willing to invest, leading to lower demand and falling prices.

Interest Rates

Interest rates, set by the Federal Reserve in the U.S., play a big role in stock prices. When interest rates are low, people are more likely to invest in stocks rather than keeping their money in savings accounts, which offer lower returns. Low interest rates often lead to higher demand for stocks. When interest rates rise, people may prefer safer investments, reducing demand for stocks and lowering prices.

News and Events

News about a company, industry, or even the economy can impact stock prices. Positive news, like a company winning a large contract or announcing a new product, can increase demand and raise the stock price. Negative news, like scandals or lawsuits, can have the opposite effect, causing people to sell and pushing the stock price down.

Investor Sentiment

Sometimes, stock prices are affected by how investors feel, even if nothing has changed within the company. If investors are optimistic about the future, they may buy stocks, driving prices up. If they're worried about potential problems, they may sell, driving prices down.

Understanding Stock Market Volatility

Because stock prices depend on supply and demand, they can change quickly, leading to volatility. Volatility is the degree to which stock prices go up or down in a short period. Some investors like volatility because it can create opportunities to buy low and sell high. However, volatility also adds risk, as it's harder to predict where prices will go.

When investing, it's important to remember that the stock market can be volatile in the short term. This means that prices may go up and down daily. However, over the long term, the stock market has generally gone up, providing growth for patient investors.

How Investors Can Respond to Price Fluctuations

As a new investor, you don't need to react to every change in stock prices. Here are some strategies for dealing with price fluctuations:

Long-Term Perspective

Many successful investors focus on the long term, holding onto stocks for years or even decades. By doing this, they avoid reacting to daily ups and downs and benefit from long-term growth.

Diversification

Diversifying means spreading your investments across different stocks, industries, or even asset types (like bonds). Diversification reduces risk because if one stock goes down, others may go up, helping balance your portfolio.

Dollar-Cost Averaging

Dollar-cost averaging involves investing a fixed amount of money at regular intervals, such as monthly. This strategy helps smooth out price fluctuations by buying more shares when prices are low and fewer shares when prices are high.

Staying Informed

Keeping up with news about your investments and the market in general can help you make better decisions. However, it's important not to overreact to every piece of news, as short-term events don't always affect a company's long-term potential.

Picking Your First Stocks

Choosing your first stocks is an exciting step in investing. It's a chance to grow your money by owning shares of companies you believe in. However, it's important to do some research before you buy. Understanding how to pick stocks based on company performance, growth potential, and market trends can help you make smarter choices. Here's a guide on how to get started with stock research, choose companies that match your goals, and understand key factors to look at.

How to Research Companies and Choose Stocks Based on Your Goals

Before buying a stock, it's helpful to set clear investment goals. Your goals can affect the types of stocks you choose. For example:

Long-Term Growth: If you're investing for retirement or want your money to grow over many years, you might look for companies with a strong history of growth.

Income from Dividends: If you want regular income from your stocks, look for companies that pay dividends, which are regular payments to shareholders.

Short-Term Gains: If you're interested in quick returns, you may want to explore growth stocks, which can rise in value quickly, though they come with higher risk.

Once you know your goals, you can start researching companies that fit. Here's how:

Pick Companies You Know or Believe In

Start by looking at companies whose products or services you understand and believe in. For example, if you like technology, you might explore tech companies. If you're interested in consumer products, consider companies that make everyday items. Knowing the business makes it easier to understand the company's potential.

Look at the Company's Basics

Research the company's main business activities, products, or services. A good place to start is the company's website, where you can find basic information about what it does, who its customers are, and what its goals are. Understanding the company's purpose helps you decide if it aligns with your goals.

Check the Company's Competitors

Look at other companies in the same industry to see how your chosen company compares. For instance, if you're looking at a technology company, check out other tech companies to see if yours stands out. Strong companies often lead their industry in sales, innovation, or market share.

The Importance of Looking at Company Earnings, Growth Potential, and Market Trends

To make a solid investment choice, it's essential to review the company's financial performance, growth potential, and the trends affecting its industry. These factors provide insight into the company's health and future prospects.

Company Earnings

Earnings are a company's profits, and they are one of the most important factors to look at when picking stocks. A company's earnings tell you how well it is doing financially.

Earnings Reports

Public companies release earnings reports every three months, also called "quarterly earnings reports." These reports show the company's revenue (total money made), expenses, and profit. You can find these reports on the company's website or financial news sites.

Look for companies with steady or growing earnings, as this shows that the business is financially healthy. Avoid companies with a history of frequent losses, as they may struggle to provide returns for investors.

Earnings Per Share (EPS)

Earnings per share (EPS) is a useful number that shows how much profit a company makes per share of its stock. You can find EPS listed on financial websites.

A higher EPS usually means the company is making more profit, which can be a good sign for investors. If a company's EPS is consistently growing, it suggests that the company is becoming more valuable.

Price-to-Earnings (P/E) Ratio

The P/E ratio compares the stock's price to its earnings. It tells you how much investors are willing to pay for each dollar of earnings. For example, a P/E ratio of 20 means investors are willing to pay $20 for every $1 the company earns.

A high P/E ratio might mean the stock is overvalued, while a low P/E ratio could indicate it's undervalued. However, P/E ratios vary by industry, so it's best to compare a company's P/E ratio to other companies in the same field.

Growth Potential

Growth potential refers to the company's ability to increase its profits and expand in the future. Here's how to assess growth potential:

Revenue Growth

Revenue growth is the increase in a company's total sales over time. Look for companies with steady revenue growth, as it shows that more people are buying their products or services.

If a company's revenue grows every year, it may mean that the company is expanding its customer base or introducing new products successfully.

Future Plans and Innovations

Check if the company has plans for new products, services, or expansions. Innovative companies with plans to grow often have better chances of increasing their profits.

You can find information about a company's future plans in its quarterly reports, annual reports, or news articles. Companies that invest in research and development (R&D) may have strong growth potential because they're always working on new things.

Industry Trends

Think about the industry the company is in and any trends that could affect it. For example, technology is a growing industry with lots of innovation, so tech companies often have high growth potential.

On the other hand, industries that rely on traditional products may grow more slowly. Researching industry trends can help you find companies that are well-positioned for the future.

Market Trends

Market trends are factors that can affect an entire industry or the economy as a whole. Understanding market trends can help you choose stocks that are likely to grow or avoid stocks that may face challenges.

Economic Trends

Economic conditions, like interest rates, inflation, and consumer spending, can impact stock prices. For example, low interest rates encourage people to invest in stocks, while high rates can reduce stock demand.

Keep an eye on news about the economy, as changes can impact stock prices. Economic growth often leads to higher stock prices, while a recession may cause prices to drop.

Technology and Innovation

Technological changes can affect many industries. For instance, advancements in digital payments have made companies like PayPal and Square more valuable. Look for companies that embrace technology and innovation, as these companies often have an edge in the market.

Environmental and Social Factors

Many investors today care about environmental and social issues, which can influence stock prices. Companies that focus on sustainability, for example, may attract more investors and see their stock price rise.

Social factors, like changing consumer preferences, can also impact companies. For example, if people start buying more electric cars, companies making them may benefit.

Steps to Pick Your First Stocks

Once you've done your research and have a few companies in mind, follow these steps to choose your first stocks:

Make a List of Potential Stocks

Start by making a list of companies that meet your goals and have good earnings, growth potential, and market trends. Choose companies from industries you understand or feel confident about.

Narrow Down the List

Look closer at each company's earnings reports, EPS, and revenue growth. Remove any companies that don't show steady growth or don't align with your goals.

Check for Diversification

Choose stocks from different industries to diversify your portfolio. For example, if you pick a tech company, consider also choosing a stock from healthcare or consumer goods. Diversification spreads risk, so you're less affected if one industry struggles.

Consider Starting Small

You don't need to invest a lot right away. Start with a small amount and add more over time. This approach lets you get comfortable with investing without taking big risks.

Monitor Your Stocks

After you buy stocks, keep an eye on the companies' earnings reports, news, and performance. However, avoid checking daily, as stock prices can fluctuate for small reasons. Monitoring helps you stay informed and decide if you want to hold onto or sell your stocks.

Long-Term Stock Market Success

Investing in the stock market is one of the most effective ways to build wealth over time. While stock prices can go up and down, the stock market has historically grown over the long run. By staying invested for many years, you give your money the chance to grow and benefit from something called *compounding*, where your earnings also start to earn returns. This is why long-term investing in the stock market has helped many people build wealth.

Why Investing in the Stock Market Builds Wealth Over Time

The stock market grows over time because companies are constantly working to expand their businesses, make new products, and improve their services. When you invest in a company by buying its stock, you become part-owner of that business. If the company does well and grows, the value of your stock increases, which means your investment grows.

Compounding Growth

Compounding is one of the most powerful reasons why long-term investing works. When you invest in stocks, you not only earn returns on your original investment but also on the returns you earn each year. Over many years, this compounding effect makes a big difference.

For example, if you invest $1,000 and it grows by 10% in a year, you'll have $1,100. The next year, you earn 10% on $1,100, not just your original $1,000, which means you'll have $1,210. Compounding helps your money grow faster over time, especially if you stay invested for decades.

Stock Market Growth Over Time

Historically, the stock market has gone up over long periods. While there are ups and downs along the way, the overall trend is positive. This is because companies grow, improve, and adapt to changing times, making their stocks more valuable.

For example, the S&P 500, an index of the 500 largest companies in the United States, has grown about 10% per year on average. This means that, historically, long-term investors have seen their money grow simply by staying invested in the market over time.

Dividends Add to Wealth

Many companies pay dividends, which are regular payments made to shareholders. Dividends are a portion of a company's profits shared with its investors. If you own a dividend-paying stock, you earn money even if the stock price doesn't go up. Many investors reinvest their dividends, meaning they use this money to buy more shares. Over time, reinvesting dividends helps increase the number of shares you own, leading to more growth.

Protection Against Inflation

Inflation means the cost of goods and services goes up over time, which reduces the value of cash savings. Stocks, however, usually grow faster than inflation. By investing in stocks, you're more likely to keep up with or even beat inflation, helping protect your wealth in the long term.

Case Studies of Successful Long-Term Stock Investors

Many investors have built significant wealth through long-term investing. Let's look at some famous examples to understand how they succeeded by staying in the market for many years.

Warren Buffett

Warren Buffett, one of the most famous investors in the world, is known for his long-term approach to investing. Buffett started investing when he was a child, and he built his wealth by holding onto stocks for many years. His company, Berkshire Hathaway, invests in businesses that have strong, stable growth.

Investment Philosophy

Mellody Hobson, co-CEO of Ariel Investments, is an inspiring example of a Black woman who has made significant contributions to the investing world. Under her leadership, Ariel Investments focuses on long-term value investing, similar to a philosophy of identifying companies with strong fundamentals and holding onto them to benefit from their growth over time.

Hobson's Investment Philosophy:

Mellody believes in investing in companies with solid leadership, a history of good performance, and products or services that align with long-term trends. Her approach includes:

- Value Investing: Identifying undervalued companies with the potential for growth.
- Patience: Holding investments for the long term to allow the power of compounding and market growth to work.
- Focus on Diversity: She also encourages companies to prioritize diversity, equity, and inclusion, recognizing that diverse teams lead to better decision-making and results.

Lesson from Hobson:

Mellody's philosophy emphasizes that investing isn't just about numbers—it's about believing in the companies you invest in and trusting that their growth will align with your financial goals. She inspires Black women to take control of their financial futures by embracing long-term investing as a tool for building wealth and creating legacies.

Examples of Long-Term Holdings

Buffett invested in companies like Coca-Cola and American Express and held onto these stocks for decades. These companies steadily grew, and so did his wealth. Buffett often says his favorite holding period is "forever," meaning he prefers to keep stocks for as long as they continue to perform well.

Lessons from Women Who Invest: Black Women Investors

Teri Ijeoma: Turning Passion into Profit

Teri Ijeoma, a prominent investor and entrepreneur, began her journey by learning how to trade stocks to create an additional income stream. Initially a school educator, Teri turned her passion for investing into a full-time career and later launched Trade and Travel, a platform that teaches others how to invest and trade.

Investment Philosophy:

Teri emphasizes the importance of education and discipline in investing. She believes that anyone can learn to invest and create financial freedom with the right tools and mindset. Teri encourages understanding the market, making informed decisions, and not being afraid to start small.

Lesson from Teri:

Start by investing in your financial education. Teri's story shows that with the right knowledge and consistent effort, it's possible to grow wealth and achieve financial independence. Her work inspires Black women to take control of their finances and explore investing as a way to reach their goals.

Mellody Hobson: Financial Literacy and Leadership

Mellody Hobson, co-CEO of Ariel Investments, is one of the most influential Black women in the financial world. She has dedicated her career to promoting financial literacy and increasing diversity in investing. Under her leadership, Ariel Investments focuses on long-term investing and has become a respected name in asset management.

Investment Philosophy:

Mellody stresses the importance of understanding the power of compound growth and starting early. She advocates for consistent, long-term investing in quality assets and encourages women to take an active role in managing their financial futures.

Lesson from Mellody:

Confidence in investing comes from knowledge and preparation. Mellody inspires women to ask questions, learn about their investments, and trust in their ability to build wealth over time.

Tiffany Aliche: The Budgetnista's Path to Wealth

Tiffany Aliche, also known as "The Budgetnista," is a financial educator who empowers women to improve their money habits and build wealth. While her focus is often on budgeting and saving, Tiffany also emphasizes the importance of investing as a tool to achieve financial independence.

Investment Philosophy:

Tiffany encourages women to start small but stay consistent. She highlights the accessibility of platforms that allow fractional investing and promotes investing in funds that align with long-term goals.

Lesson from Tiffany:

You don't have to start with a lot of money to invest. By taking small, consistent steps and prioritizing financial education, you can create a solid foundation for long-term growth.

These women show that investing isn't limited to the wealthy or those with financial degrees. They have all carved their paths in the investing world, emphasizing education, long-term thinking, and empowering others to take charge of their financial futures. Their stories serve as an inspiration to Black women looking to build wealth and create lasting legacies.

How to Apply These Lessons to Your Own Investing

These investors show that long-term success comes from patience, understanding your investments, and making simple choices that match your goals. Here are some tips for applying these lessons:

Be Patient

Investing is a marathon, not a sprint. The stock market has ups and downs, but over time, it tends to go up. By staying invested for the long term, you give your money the chance to grow through compounding.

Invest in What You Know

Look for companies whose products or services you understand and believe in. When you know a company well, you'll feel more confident in your investment, making it easier to stick with it over time.

Consider Index Funds

If you're unsure about picking individual stocks, consider investing in an index fund. Index funds give you exposure to a broad range of companies, providing growth with less risk. This is a simple way to benefit from the stock market's overall growth.

Reinvest Dividends

If you invest in dividend-paying stocks, consider reinvesting those dividends to buy more shares. This increases your investment over time and helps your money grow faster through compounding.

Stay Informed but Avoid Overreacting

It's good to stay informed about the companies you invest in, but avoid reacting to every piece of news. Stock prices can change for small reasons, but staying calm and focused on the long term helps you make better decisions.

Chapter 9

Building Wealth with Passive Income Investments

What is Passive Income?

Building wealth is often a long-term goal, and one of the most effective ways to reach it is by creating streams of *passive income*. Passive income is money you earn with little to no ongoing work after the initial setup. This means once you've set up a passive income source, it can keep generating money for you, which can help you build wealth over time.

Passive income is income that requires little effort to maintain once it's up and running. It's not like a regular job, where you have to work a set number of hours to get paid. Instead, passive income lets you earn money even while you're sleeping, traveling, or focusing on other things.

Initial Setup

Most types of passive income need an initial investment of either time, money, or both. For example, you might need to save up money to buy stocks that pay dividends or spend time creating an online product that you can sell over and over again. After this initial effort, passive income requires minimal work to keep going.

Examples of Passive Income

Some common examples of passive income include rental income from real estate, dividends from stocks, interest from savings accounts or bonds, royalties from books or music, and revenue from an online business. These income sources continue to bring in money with little day-to-day effort.

Why Passive Income is Valuable

Passive income helps build wealth because it doesn't rely on you trading your time for money. Instead, you set up income streams that can keep growing and paying you. The more passive income sources you have, the more money you can earn without needing to actively work for it. Passive income can also provide financial security and freedom, allowing you to spend more time on things you enjoy.

How Passive Income Investments Build Wealth Over Time

Passive income investments grow wealth over time by steadily increasing the money you earn. Here's how different types of passive income can work together to build your wealth:

Compounding Growth

Many passive income sources, like dividends and interest, benefit from compounding growth. This means that the income you earn can be reinvested to earn even more income. Over time, this creates a snowball effect where your money grows faster and faster.

Diversification of Income Sources

When you have multiple streams of passive income, you're less dependent on any single source of money. This is called diversification. For example, if you have both dividend-paying stocks and rental income, you're not relying only on one form of income. This reduces risk and gives you a more stable financial foundation.

Tax Advantages in the U.S.

In the U.S., some types of passive income come with tax benefits. For example, dividends from qualified stocks are taxed at a lower rate than regular income, and rental property owners can often deduct expenses like mortgage interest and property taxes. By taking advantage of these tax benefits, you can keep more of your passive income and grow your wealth faster.

Financial Freedom and Security

Passive income provides a sense of financial freedom because you're earning money without having to actively work for it. Over time, building enough passive income can help you reach financial independence, where your income from investments covers your living expenses. This can provide security and open up opportunities to pursue hobbies, travel, or even retire early.

Types of Passive Income Investments

There are several ways to earn passive income in the U.S., each with its own benefits and challenges. Here are some of the most popular types of passive income investments:

Dividend Stocks

Dividend stocks are shares in companies that pay a portion of their profits to shareholders in the form of dividends. By investing in dividend stocks, you can receive regular payments, typically every quarter.

How It Works:

When you buy shares of a company that pays dividends, you earn a portion of the company's profits. For example, if a company pays a dividend of $2 per share and you own 100 shares, you would receive $200 annually.

Benefits:

Dividends can be reinvested to buy more shares, increasing your income over time. Additionally, dividends are taxed at a lower rate than regular income in the U.S., making them a tax-efficient way to earn passive income.

Risks:

Not all companies pay dividends, and dividend payments can be reduced or stopped if the company isn't doing well.

Rental Properties

Owning rental properties is one of the most common ways to earn passive income. When you own a property and rent it out, you receive rental income each month.

How It Works:

You buy a property, find tenants, and collect rent from them each month. Ideally, the rent covers your mortgage, taxes, maintenance, and other costs, with some profit left over.

Benefits:

Rental income provides steady cash flow, and property values usually increase over time, which means you might also make money if you sell the property later. In the U.S., landlords can also deduct expenses like mortgage interest and property taxes, which reduces their taxable income.

Risks:
Rental properties require management, which can take time and effort, especially if tenants have issues. There's also a risk that property values might go down, or you could have trouble finding tenants.

Real Estate Investment Trusts (REITs)

REITs allow you to invest in real estate without owning property directly. A REIT is a company that owns or finances income-producing real estate, such as shopping centers, office buildings, or apartments.

How It Works:
When you buy shares in a REIT, you earn a portion of the rental income the REIT collects. REITs are traded on the stock exchange, so you can buy and sell shares easily.

Benefits:
REITs pay high dividends, providing a steady income without the need to manage property. They're also more liquid than rental properties, meaning you can sell your shares quickly if needed.

Risks:
REITs depend on the performance of the real estate market, so their value can go up and down. REIT dividends are also taxed at a higher rate than qualified stock dividends.

Peer-to-Peer Lending

Peer-to-peer (P2P) lending is a way to earn interest by lending money to individuals or small businesses through online platforms. Borrowers pay back the loan with interest, and you earn passive income from these interest payments.

How It Works:
You use a P2P lending platform to lend money directly to borrowers. They pay back the loan with interest, which becomes your passive income.

Benefits:
P2P lending can offer high returns, depending on the interest rate set by the platform. It's also flexible, as you can choose how much to lend and to whom.

Risks:
Borrowers might default (fail to pay back), which means you could lose money. P2P lending is also less regulated than traditional banks, so there's more risk involved.

High-Yield Savings Accounts and Bonds

While savings accounts and bonds are low-risk investments, they offer a passive way to earn income through interest.
How It Works:
A high-yield savings account pays a higher interest rate than regular savings accounts, and bonds pay you interest over a set period.
Benefits:
Savings accounts and bonds are low risk, providing steady, predictable returns. They're also easy to access if you need cash quickly.
Risks:
Returns are lower compared to stocks or rental income. Inflation can also erode the value of interest earned, meaning your purchasing power may decrease over time.

How to Get Started with Passive Income Investments

Starting with passive income investments requires some planning and research. Here are some basic steps to help you begin:

Define Your Goals

Decide what you want to achieve with passive income. Are you looking for steady monthly income, or do you want long-term growth? Knowing your goals can help you pick the right investments.

Start Small and Diversify

If you're new to investing, consider starting small and diversifying. You don't need to put all your money in one place. Try a mix of dividend stocks, a high-yield savings account, and maybe some REITs to spread your risk.

Consider Tax Implications

Be aware of the tax rules for each type of passive income. For example, dividends and REIT income may be taxed differently, and rental properties offer certain deductions. Consulting with a tax advisor can help you understand how to maximize tax benefits.

Stay Informed

Monitor your investments to make sure they're meeting your goals. While passive income doesn't need constant attention, checking in on your investments periodically can help you adjust as needed.

Types of Passive Income Investments

Passive income is money you earn without needing to work for it regularly. After setting it up, a passive income investment can keep paying you over time, which makes it a valuable way to build wealth. Let's look at different types of passive income investments, including dividend-paying stocks, real estate, peer-to-peer lending, and more. We'll also discuss how to balance passive income with active investments.

Dividend-Paying Stocks

Dividend-paying stocks are shares in companies that pay a portion of their profits to shareholders as dividends. These are regular payments you receive just for owning the stock, usually every quarter.

How It Works:

When you buy shares in a company that pays dividends, you receive money each time the company makes a profit and decides to share it with its investors. For example, if a company pays $1 per share each quarter and you own 100 shares, you'd earn $100 every quarter.

Benefits:

Dividends provide a steady income without needing to sell your shares. You can either keep the money or reinvest it to buy more shares, which can grow your income over time.

Risks:

Not all companies pay dividends, and those that do can reduce or stop payments if they're not making enough money. It's important to choose stable companies with a history of paying dividends.

Dividend stocks are a popular way to build passive income because they don't need much management, and many companies increase dividends over time, growing your income.

Real Estate (Rental Income)

Real estate, especially rental properties, is a well-known source of passive income. By owning property and renting it out to tenants, you can receive regular rental income each month.

How It Works:

You buy a property, like a house or an apartment, and rent it out to tenants. Each month, they pay you rent, which becomes your income. Ideally, the rent covers the mortgage, taxes, maintenance, and other costs, with some left over as profit.

Benefits:

Rental properties provide steady cash flow, and properties can increase in value over time, giving you more potential profit if you decide to sell.

Risks:

Managing property and tenants takes time and effort, and there's always a chance that you might not find tenants quickly. There's also a risk of property value going down in a bad market.

While real estate can require some management, it offers both income and long-term value growth, making it a good choice for many passive income seekers.

Peer-to-Peer Lending

Peer-to-peer (P2P) lending is a way to earn passive income by lending money directly to individuals or small businesses through online platforms. When borrowers pay back the loan with interest, you earn income.

How It Works:

You lend money to borrowers on a P2P platform, which matches you with people who need a loan. The borrowers pay back the loan in instalments with interest, and that interest is your income.

Benefits:

P2P lending can offer higher interest rates compared to traditional savings accounts, giving you more income on your investment.

Risks:

There's a chance that borrowers might not repay their loans, which could mean losing some of your money. P2P lending is less regulated than banks, which can make it riskier.

P2P lending is a flexible way to earn passive income, but it's important to lend carefully and diversify by lending small amounts to multiple borrowers instead of one large loan.

High-Yield Savings Accounts

High-yield savings accounts pay a higher interest rate than regular savings accounts, making them a simple way to earn passive income without taking on much risk.

How It Works:

You deposit money in a high-yield savings account, and the bank pays you interest regularly. While the interest rate is lower than other investments, it's a safe and steady option.

Benefits:

High-yield savings accounts are low risk and easily accessible, which makes them useful for short-term savings and emergency funds.

Risks:

The income is lower than other investments, and inflation can reduce the purchasing power of the money in your account.

A high-yield savings account is a good choice for low-risk income, but it won't generate as much income as stocks or real estate.

Real Estate Investment Trusts (REITs)

A Real Estate Investment Trust, or REIT, is a company that owns or manages real estate properties. By buying shares in a REIT, you can earn income from real estate without owning property directly.

How It Works:

When you invest in a REIT, you earn a portion of the income the REIT makes from its properties, like rental income from shopping centers or office buildings. REITs are traded on stock exchanges, so they're easy to buy and sell.

Benefits:

REITs provide high dividends and are easier to manage than rental properties. They're also more liquid, meaning you can sell your shares easily if you need cash.

Risks:

REITs depend on the real estate market, so their value can fluctuate. Dividends from REITs are often taxed as regular income, which is higher than capital gains taxes on stocks.

REITs are a good option for those who want to invest in real estate without managing properties. They offer regular income and are easy to buy and sell.

Balancing Passive Income with Active Investments

Balancing passive income with active investments helps you grow your wealth in a balanced way. Here's how you can do it:

Set Your Goals

Decide how much income you want from passive sources. For example, you might want passive income to cover monthly expenses, or you might want it for long-term savings. Knowing your goals can help you decide how much to invest in passive income sources versus active investments like stocks that you trade more frequently.

Diversify Your Income Streams

Don't rely on just one type of passive income. Diversifying means investing in different sources, like dividend stocks, rental income, and REITs. This spreads risk and makes your income more stable.

Balance Risk and Return

Passive income sources, like high-yield savings accounts, are low risk but have lower returns. Others, like real estate or P2P lending, offer higher returns but carry more risk. Balance low-risk sources with higher-risk ones to manage your overall risk and increase returns.

Consider Tax Implications

Different investments have different tax rules. For example, dividends are taxed at a lower rate than ordinary income, while P2P interest income may be taxed at a higher rate. Knowing the tax effects can help you decide where to invest to keep more of your income.

Reinvest for Growth

Reinvesting passive income can help it grow faster. For example, you can reinvest dividends to buy more shares or use rental income to buy another property. Reinvesting helps your income increase without adding more money from your savings.

Adjust Over Time

As you get closer to your financial goals, adjust your balance between passive and active investments. You might want more stable passive income as you get older and rely less on active investments.

Creating a Passive Income Strategy

Creating a passive income strategy is about building income sources that continue to earn money without much daily work. By carefully choosing investments and reinvesting earnings, you can grow your wealth faster over time.

How to Identify the Best Passive Income Investments for Your Portfolio

Finding the best passive income investments depends on what you want to achieve, your budget, and how much risk you're comfortable taking. Here are some steps to help you choose the right investments:

Know Your Financial Goals

Start by thinking about your goals for passive income. Do you want steady monthly income to help pay bills? Or are you looking for long-term growth to build a nest egg? For regular income, consider dividend stocks or rental property. For long-term growth, you might focus on investments that reinvest earnings, like Real Estate Investment Trusts (REITs) or high-growth stocks.

Consider Risk Levels

Different types of passive income investments come with different risks. Dividend stocks are relatively stable but can still fluctuate. REITs and rental properties have the potential for high returns but also come with market risks. High-yield savings accounts are very safe but don't offer much growth. Choose a balance of investments to spread risk and keep your portfolio stable.

Think About Taxes

In the U.S., different passive income types have different tax rules. For example, qualified dividends from certain stocks are taxed at a lower rate than regular income. Real estate owners can also benefit from tax deductions on mortgage interest and property taxes. Understanding these tax benefits can help you choose the most tax-efficient options for your income goals.

Select Investment Types

Based on your goals, budget, risk tolerance, and tax considerations, you can start building your portfolio. Below are common passive income options to consider:

Dividend-Paying Stocks

These are shares in companies that pay a portion of their profits to shareholders regularly. They are ideal for generating steady income and can be reinvested to grow your investment further.

Real Estate (Rental Properties)

Owning properties that you rent out to tenants provides a reliable cash flow. Additionally, property values often increase over time, making this a strong choice for wealth-building.

Real Estate Investment Trusts (REITs)

REITs are companies that own income-generating real estate. They offer high dividends and allow you to invest in real estate without directly owning property, making them an accessible option for many investors.

Peer-to-Peer Lending

This involves lending money to individuals or small businesses through online platforms. As borrowers repay their loans, you earn interest, creating a source of passive income.

High-Yield Savings Accounts and Bonds

These are safe and stable investments that provide interest income. While they don't offer rapid growth, they are dependable and provide easy access to cash when needed.

Tips for Reinvesting Your Passive Income to Grow Your Wealth Faster

Once you start earning passive income, reinvesting can help you grow your wealth even faster. Here are some ways to make the most of your earnings:

Reinvest Dividends

If you're investing in dividend-paying stocks or REITs, consider reinvesting the dividends to buy more shares. Many brokers offer automatic dividend reinvestment plans (DRIPs) that use your dividends to purchase additional shares. This approach helps you increase the number of shares you own, leading to more dividend income in the future.

Use Rental Income for Property Improvements

For rental properties, consider using part of your rental income to make improvements to the property. Upgrades can increase the property's value and attract higher-paying tenants, which can grow your rental income over time. This reinvestment can also help your property appreciate faster, making it a stronger long-term asset.

Buy More of the Same Investments

If you're comfortable with your current investments, reinvesting income to buy more of the same assets can build your portfolio quickly. For example, if you earn interest from bonds or peer-to-peer lending, you can use that income to buy more bonds or make more loans, increasing your income potential.

Diversify into New Passive Income Streams

Diversifying helps protect your income and reduces risk. If you're earning passive income from dividend stocks, for example, consider using some of that income to invest in a REIT or high-yield savings account. This way, if one source slows down, you still have other income streams.

Take Advantage of Compound Interest

Compound interest is when you earn interest not only on your original investment but also on the earnings it generates. For example, in a high-yield savings account, your balance grows as you earn interest, and each new interest payment is calculated on a larger balance. Reinvesting passive income lets you benefit from compounding, which speeds up wealth growth.

Automate Reinvestment

Many brokerage accounts allow you to automate reinvestment, which makes the process easier and ensures that your money is constantly working for you. Set up automatic reinvestment for dividends, interest, or rental income to maximize your returns without extra effort.

Increase Investments When Possible

If you receive a raise, a bonus, or unexpected income, consider adding it to your passive income investments. Increasing your investment over time boosts your returns and helps you reach your financial goals faster.

Regularly Review Your Strategy

As your financial situation changes, it's a good idea to review and adjust your passive income strategy. For example, if you're nearing retirement, you may want to shift toward safer investments that provide steady income, like bonds or high-dividend stocks. Regularly reviewing your strategy keeps your portfolio aligned with your goals and risk tolerance.

Chapter 10

Investing In Yourself

The Power of Personal Development

Investing in yourself means putting time, effort, and sometimes money into developing your skills, knowledge, and well-being. This kind of investment builds personal "wealth" because it makes you a stronger, more capable person. Whether you're learning something new, improving your health, or building good habits, investing in yourself is a smart way to grow.

The Power of Personal Development

Personal development is all about improving yourself in ways that make you happier, healthier, and more skilled. When you invest in your own growth, you build a foundation that supports everything else in your life, including your career, finances, and relationships. Here's how it works:

Building Lasting Value

When you improve your skills or knowledge, that knowledge stays with you. Skills like problem-solving, communication, or even technical skills don't just disappear—they stay with you for life. This lasting value makes you more capable, helping you handle challenges and take advantage of opportunities that come your way.

Increasing Confidence and Self-Worth

Learning something new or achieving a personal goal boosts your confidence. Each time you succeed, it reinforces your belief in yourself, making you more willing to try new things and take on bigger challenges. Confidence helps you communicate better, make decisions, and pursue your dreams with energy and focus.

Setting Yourself Apart in the Job Market

Developing your skills and knowledge makes you stand out in a competitive job market. When employers see that you're continuously improving, they're more likely to view you as a valuable employee. For example, learning a new technology, improving a skill, or earning a certification shows that you're serious about growing and contributing to the company.

Health as a Key Investment

Personal development also includes your physical and mental health. When you exercise, eat well, and get enough rest, you're investing in your own energy and focus. Good health makes it easier to stay productive and do your best. Taking care of your mental health through relaxation, hobbies, or meditation helps reduce stress and keeps you feeling balanced.

Personal Development is Compounding

Similar to how compound interest grows your money, investing in yourself has a compounding effect. Each new skill you learn or habit you build adds to what you already know, creating a stronger foundation for future success. The more you grow, the more you can achieve, creating a cycle of continuous improvement.

How Continuous Learning and Skill-Building Can Increase Your Income Potential

Learning and improving your skills is one of the best ways to increase your income over time. When you know more and can do more, you become more valuable in any job or business. Here's how continuous learning can help you earn more:

Developing In-Demand Skills

Different careers require different skills, but some skills are always in demand. For example, technology skills like coding, data analysis, or digital marketing are valuable in many fields. By learning these high-demand skills, you increase your chances of finding better-paying jobs or opportunities. When employers need people with specific skills, they're often willing to pay more for that expertise.

Advancing in Your Career

Continuous learning can open doors to promotions and new responsibilities. In many careers, people who learn and improve are the ones who get promoted. For example, a person who takes the time to learn leadership skills might become a manager or team leader. With each promotion, your income potential grows.

Increasing Your Value with Certifications

Many industries have certifications or special qualifications that show you're skilled in a particular area. Earning these certifications can boost your income potential because it proves to employers that you have the skills they need. For example, a project manager with a PMP (Project Management Professional) certification is often paid more than one without it.

Learning to Start Your Own Business or Side Income

Learning new skills can also help you start your own business or a side income. For example, if you take a course on graphic design, you might start a side business creating designs for clients. Similarly, learning marketing or finance can help you start a small business or become a freelancer. Having a side income increases your overall earning power and makes you more financially secure.

Adapting to Changes in the Job Market

The job market is always changing, with new jobs and skills emerging. Continuous learning helps you stay updated and ready for these changes. For example, as technology advances, more jobs require knowledge of digital tools or coding. By keeping up with these trends, you make sure that your skills remain valuable, increasing your ability to find good job opportunities.

Practical Ways to Invest in Yourself

Investing in yourself doesn't have to be complicated or expensive. Here are some simple, practical ways to start:

Reading Books or Taking Online Courses

Books and online courses are affordable ways to learn new skills or improve existing ones. There are courses on nearly every topic, from business to cooking to creative writing. Platforms like Coursera, Udemy, and LinkedIn Learning offer quality courses that you can take at your own pace.

Attending Workshops or Webinars

Workshops and webinars are great for learning specific skills in a short time. Many of these events are free or low-cost and offer a hands-on approach to learning. Topics might include time management, financial literacy, or public speaking. These skills can make a big difference in your personal and professional life.

Networking and Building Connection

Meeting people in your field or industry helps you learn from others' experiences and opens doors to new opportunities. Networking events, conferences, or even online groups can help you connect with people who share your interests. Having a strong network of contacts can help you learn faster, find jobs, and grow in your career.

Focusing on Health and Well-being

Good health is essential for productivity and focus. Simple changes, like eating balanced meals, exercising regularly, and getting enough sleep, can make a big difference in your energy levels. Practicing mindfulness or meditation can reduce stress and improve mental health. Investing in health is an important part of personal growth because it gives you the strength to pursue your goals.

Setting Personal Goals and Tracking Progress

Setting goals helps you stay focused and motivated. For example, you might set a goal to read one book a month or complete an online course within three months. Tracking your progress keeps you motivated and helps you see the results of your efforts, which makes you feel accomplished.

Practicing Skills Regularly

Practice is key to mastering any skill. Whether it's writing, public speaking, or computer programming, regular practice makes you better over time. Setting aside even 15–30 minutes a day to practice a skill can lead to big improvements. Over time, these small steps add up and make you more skilled and confident.

Networking and Building Connections

Networking is the process of meeting people, building relationships, and creating connections that can help you in your career, investments, and financial growth. A strong network doesn't just consist of knowing a lot of people but involves having meaningful connections that add real value to your life. When you connect with people who are supportive and knowledgeable, you gain access to more opportunities and resources, which can make a big difference.

How to Leverage Your Network

A well-built network is like planting seeds that can grow into valuable resources. When you build relationships, stay in touch, and support others, your network can offer you opportunities in different areas of life.

One powerful benefit of networking is finding investment opportunities. People in your network may know about investments that aren't widely advertised. For example, a friend might hear about a startup seeking early investors or a real estate opportunity before it goes public. Connecting with people who actively invest can give you access to these opportunities and allow you to learn from their experiences. When you have friends or mentors who are skilled in investing, they can help you understand the risks and benefits of different investments, giving you a better chance at making wise choices.

Another benefit of networking is learning from the experiences of others. People in your network have their own unique paths, full of successes and mistakes. By listening to their stories, you can gain valuable insights into what works and what doesn't. For instance, if someone shares a story about losing money on a risky investment, you can learn from their experience and avoid similar mistakes. On the other hand, if they made a profit from a smart investment, you can try to understand what factors contributed to that success.

Networking also opens doors for career advancement. Many job opportunities and promotions come from referrals or recommendations from people who know your work. When you build a strong network, people are more likely to recommend you for roles that match your skills. Often, job openings aren't even posted online because companies fill them quickly through referrals. Staying connected with people in your industry helps you stay on their radar, increasing your chances of being recommended when these hidden opportunities arise.

Learning new skills and knowledge is another advantage of networking. By interacting with others in your field, you can learn valuable tips and strategies. For example, you might meet someone who is skilled in budgeting or public speaking, and through casual conversation, you pick up useful advice. This ongoing exchange of knowledge helps you grow, both personally and professionally, by learning from others' expertise.

Networking can also help you find business partners or collaborators if you're interested in starting a business. Suppose you have a great idea for a product but lack marketing skills. By networking, you might meet someone with the skills you need to turn your idea into a reality. Working with people who have different strengths can create a balanced team, which is essential for business success. A strong team brings diverse perspectives and makes it easier to overcome challenges.

Lastly, networking allows you to build a reputation as a reliable and helpful contact. Networking isn't just about what you can get from others; it's also about what you can give. When you support people in your network, they're more likely to remember you positively and may share opportunities with you in the future. Being a reliable contact and helping others builds a reputation that encourages people to connect with you and share valuable information or opportunities.

The Value of Mentorship and Surrounding Yourself with Financially Savvy Individuals

Having mentors and financially knowledgeable friends is like having a "success team" to help guide you toward your goals. These people bring experience, knowledge, and insights that can make a big difference in your financial life and personal development.

Mentors are people who have more experience and can offer advice and guidance. They've often been where you are and understand the challenges you might face. A good mentor can share lessons from their journey, helping you avoid mistakes and make better decisions. For example, if you're new to investing, a mentor with financial expertise can teach you the basics and guide you toward safer options. They can also provide encouragement and support, especially when you're learning or facing challenges.

Financially knowledgeable friends and mentors can also provide honest feedback. If you're considering an investment, they might help you weigh the risks and benefits, giving you a different perspective that can prevent impulsive or risky decisions. These friends and mentors can also point out areas where you can improve financially. For instance, they may suggest better budgeting methods, ways to save more, or strategies to increase your income. Honest feedback from trusted people helps you grow and make smarter financial choices.

Having financially knowledgeable friends and mentors also means gaining access to valuable resources and information. These individuals often know about tools, books, courses, and websites that can help you improve your financial skills. For example, a financially savvy friend might recommend a budgeting app that helps you track expenses, or a mentor might introduce you to a reliable investment website. This access to resources and up-to-date information keeps you informed and prepared for financial opportunities.

Financial growth can sometimes be challenging, and setbacks are common. Having supportive people around you makes it easier to stay motivated and keep pushing forward. Friends and mentors who understand financial growth can offer encouragement when things get tough. For example, if you face a setback, like losing money on an investment, they can reassure you that it's part of the learning process and encourage you to keep trying. This support can make a huge difference in keeping you committed to your financial journey.

Surrounding yourself with financially knowledgeable people also helps you pick up smart financial habits. Watching how these friends and mentors handle their money can inspire you to adopt similar habits, such as saving regularly, budgeting effectively, or investing wisely. Good financial habits, like building an emergency fund and avoiding unnecessary debt, help create a strong financial foundation. By learning these habits from people who practice them, you start making better choices and improving your own financial health.

Lastly, financially savvy mentors and friends can help expand your network even further. They often know other people who are skilled or knowledgeable, and they may introduce you to them. These introductions can open up even more opportunities, allowing you to keep building your network and benefiting from a larger circle of support and resources.

Finding Balance

Building wealth and taking care of your personal well-being are both important. However, it's easy to focus so much on one that you neglect the other. Finding a good balance between financial investments, personal growth, and health helps you create a happy, healthy, and secure future.

How to Balance Financial Investments with Personal Growth and Health

Investing in your future is essential, but so is taking care of yourself. If you focus only on financial investments, you might end up tired, stressed, and unable to enjoy the rewards of your hard work. Similarly, focusing solely on personal growth and health without planning for financial security could lead to stress later in life. Here are some key ways to keep a good balance:

Set Clear Goals for Both Finances and Personal Well-Being

Start by setting goals for both your financial life and your personal life. For example, a financial goal might be to save for retirement, while a personal goal might be to stay healthy and stress-free. Setting these goals helps you prioritize both areas, making sure that you pay attention to each.

Understand Your Values and Priorities

Think about what matters most to you. Are you more focused on achieving financial freedom, or do you value spending time on hobbies, family, and personal growth? Knowing what's most important helps you make decisions that match your values. For example, if family time is very important, you might choose a job with a lower salary but better work-life balance.

Create a Balanced Budget

Your budget can include both financial investments and spending on personal growth or health. Set aside money for investments, like stocks or savings, but also plan for personal expenses, like gym memberships, classes, or vacations. This way, you're building wealth while also investing in your well-being.

Include Personal Goals in Your Financial Plans

Personal goals often need financial support. For instance, if you want to improve your health, you may need money for exercise equipment or healthy groceries. Including personal goals in your financial plan makes it easier to support both your finances and your health.

Limit Stress by Avoiding Overcommitment

Sometimes, trying to do everything at once leads to burnout. Avoid committing to too many goals or taking on more than you can handle financially. Instead, start with small steps, whether you're saving a little each month or exercising for a few minutes daily. Gradual progress in both areas helps you avoid feeling overwhelmed.

Separate Work and Personal Time

It's important to create boundaries between work, financial planning, and personal life. Set aside specific times for each so that you're not constantly thinking about work or investments. When it's time for personal activities, fully enjoy them without distractions. This way, you can recharge, making it easier to focus on finances when needed.

Practical Tips for Budgeting Time and Money for Both Personal and Financial Investments

Balancing time and money between finances, personal growth, and health requires careful planning. Here are some practical tips to help you budget for both:

Create a "Time Budget" Just Like a Money Budget

Just as you budget money, you can budget your time. For instance, set aside time each day for work, financial planning, exercise, and relaxation. This helps you make sure you're spending time on all the things that matter, without letting one area dominate. Setting a specific time for activities, like working out in the morning or checking finances on weekends, keeps you organized and balanced.

Set Up Separate Funds for Financial Goals and Personal Goals

Having separate funds for financial investments and personal goals keeps your budget organized. For example, you might have an investment fund for stocks and a separate wellness fund for gym fees or personal development courses. This way, you can track both areas without mixing them, making it easier to see your progress in each.

Schedule Regular "Check-ins" for Your Goals

Set aside time each month to check on your financial goals and personal goals. This can be as simple as reviewing your budget and tracking how much you've saved or invested. For personal goals, check if you're keeping up with exercise, relaxation, or other activities that support your well-being. Regular check-ins help you stay on track and make adjustments as needed.

Plan Time for Rest and Recovery

Rest and relaxation are essential for staying healthy and focused. When planning your time, include moments to rest and unwind, even if it's just a few minutes each day. Avoid overloading your schedule with work or financial tasks so that you have time to recharge. Regular breaks prevent burnout and make it easier to stay committed to both your financial and personal goals.

Set Short-Term Goals to Build Confidence

Short-term goals help you build confidence and stay motivated. For finances, a short-term goal might be saving a small amount each week. For personal growth, it might be reading a chapter of a self-improvement book daily. Achieving these small goals makes you feel accomplished, which encourages you to keep working toward your larger goals.

Automate Financial Contributions for Peace of Mind

Automation helps you invest without thinking about it daily. For example, you can set up automatic transfers to savings or retirement accounts each month. This way, your investments grow automatically, while you focus on other areas of your life. Automating finances reduces stress and makes it easier to maintain a balance.

Use Apps to Manage Your Time and Money

Apps can make budgeting and time management easier. Budgeting apps, like Mint or YNAB, help you track spending, set goals, and see where your money goes. Time management apps, like Google Calendar or Todoist, help you organize your schedule, so you're balancing both financial and personal goals.

Reward Yourself for Achieving Goals

Rewards can motivate you to keep working toward your goals. When you reach a financial goal, like saving a set amount, treat yourself with something small, like a nice meal or a new book. For personal goals, you could reward yourself after consistently working out for a month. Rewards make the process enjoyable and help you look forward to achieving more.

Prioritize Health as a Long-Term Investment

Health is an investment that supports everything else in your life. Prioritize exercise, healthy eating, and sleep as part of your budget, just like you would for financial investments. When you're healthy, you have more energy to work on financial goals and enjoy personal time. This investment in health pays off over time as it helps prevent medical costs and improves your quality of life.

Keep Learning for Continuous Growth

Learning is part of both personal and financial growth. Read books, take courses, or attend workshops that help you improve skills and make smarter financial choices. For example, learning about budgeting can help you manage money better, while a fitness course can teach you exercises to stay active. Continuous learning keeps you improving in all areas of life.

Avoid Comparing Yourself to Others

It's easy to feel pressured by others' achievements, but everyone's path is unique. Focus on your own goals and progress without comparing yourself to others. This helps you enjoy your achievements and stay motivated on your own journey. Balancing life isn't about matching others; it's about finding what works best for you.

Chapter 11

Teaching Financial Literacy To The Next Generation

Why Financial Education Matters

Teaching financial literacy to younger generations is a powerful way to help them succeed and create a stable future. Financial literacy means understanding how money works—how to earn, save, spend, and invest it wisely. When we pass on financial knowledge to children and young people, we give them the tools they need to make good financial decisions throughout life.

Financial education is important because money plays a big role in every part of life. From buying basic necessities to planning for the future, money decisions are part of everyday life. By teaching financial literacy to the next generation, we help them make smarter choices that can lead to financial stability and independence. Here are some key reasons why financial education matters:

Developing Good Money Habits Early

When children learn about money from an early age, they're more likely to develop good habits. Simple lessons like saving a part of their allowance or learning to budget for a toy teach them that money is a resource that needs to be managed. Starting with small habits helps them grow up with a responsible approach to money, which becomes second nature as they grow older.

Preparing for Real-World Decisions

Financial literacy prepares young people for real-world decisions, such as choosing a career, buying a car, or paying for college. If they don't know how to manage money, they may end up making costly mistakes, like taking on unnecessary debt. By learning how to budget, save, and spend wisely, they can make better choices that set them up for a secure future.

Avoiding Financial Stress

Financial problems are one of the biggest causes of stress for people. When young people understand how to manage money, they're less likely to experience this stress as adults. Knowing how to save for emergencies and avoid debt helps them feel more in control of their finances, reducing anxiety and improving mental health.

Building Financial Confidence

When young people understand money, they feel more confident about their financial decisions. This confidence empowers them to make smart choices, like investing, starting a business, or buying a home. Financial confidence also makes them less likely to fall for scams or make impulsive financial decisions.

Encouraging Responsibility

Teaching financial literacy encourages responsibility. When children learn that their financial choices have consequences, they become more thoughtful about their actions. For example, if they save money for a new game, they understand the value of patience and planning. This sense of responsibility is important not only for finances but for life in general.

How Teaching Financial Literacy Can Break Generational Cycles of Debt

Many families struggle with debt, which can create a cycle passed down through generations. This happens when parents who don't understand finances teach their children, even unintentionally, the same poor financial habits. By educating young people about money, we can help break this cycle and create a better future for them. Here's how teaching financial literacy can make a difference:

Understanding Debt and How to Avoid It

When young people understand how debt works, they're more cautious about borrowing money. They learn about interest rates, which is the extra money paid back on top of a loan, and how debt can grow if it's not managed carefully. For example, if someone borrows $1,000 with a high-interest rate, they may end up paying much more over the long term. Knowing this helps young people avoid unnecessary debt and manage any debt they do take on.

Learning to Save for Goals Instead of Borrowing

Many people borrow money to pay for things they want, which can lead to debt. By teaching young people to save for their goals, we help them understand that they don't always need to borrow. For example, if they want a new phone, they can save a little each month instead of putting it on a credit card. Saving for goals teaches patience and prevents the need for debt.

Creating an Emergency Fund

One of the biggest causes of debt is unexpected expenses, like car repairs or medical bills. Teaching young people to save a small amount for emergencies helps them avoid borrowing when something unexpected happens. An emergency fund gives them a safety net, so they're prepared and don't need to rely on loans or credit cards.

Budgeting to Live Within Their Means

Living within your means not spending more than you earn. When young people learn to budget, they understand how to balance income and expenses. This prevents the need for borrowing to cover everyday costs. For example, if they earn $500 a month, they learn to plan their spending to fit within that amount. Budgeting skills help them avoid overspending and build financial security.

Understanding the Benefits of Investing

Investing is a powerful way to build wealth, but many people never learn how to do it. Teaching young people the basics of investing, like stocks and bonds, helps them understand how their money can grow over time. Even small investments can grow significantly with time. For example, a small amount invested at age 20 can be worth much more by retirement age due to compound growth, where they earn returns on their returns. Learning this early encourages them to invest instead of relying on debt.

Practical Tips for Teaching Financial Literacy to the Next Generation

Teaching financial literacy doesn't have to be complicated. Here are some simple and practical ways to pass on these skills to young people:

Start with Small Lessons

Begin with easy lessons that fit their age. For young children, this might be learning to save part of their allowance in a piggy bank. For teenagers, it could mean helping them create a simple budget. Small steps introduce financial concepts in a way that's easy to understand.

Use Real-Life Examples

Real-life examples make financial lessons more relatable. For example, if you're grocery shopping, explain how you compare prices to save money. If you're planning a vacation, show them how you budget for it. These everyday situations help them see how financial decisions are part of daily life.

Teach the Value of Saving and Delayed Gratification

Saving teaches patience and helps young people avoid impulse buying. Encourage them to save for something they want, like a toy or game, instead of buying it right away. This lesson in delayed gratification shows them that saving for something makes it more meaningful and enjoyable.

Introduce the Basics of Investing

For older children or teens, introduce simple investing concepts. Explain how money grows over time with compound interest. You could use examples, like explaining that a $100 investment can grow over the years. Teaching the basics of investing helps them see the long-term benefits of saving and investing.

Encourage Responsibility with an Allowance

An allowance can be a great way to teach money management. Give them a small weekly or monthly amount, and let them decide how to spend or save it. This helps them understand budgeting, planning, and making choices with limited money.

Explain How to Use Credit Wisely

Credit can be a helpful tool if used carefully, but it can also lead to debt if not managed well. Teach young people about credit cards, interest rates, and the importance of paying on time. Explain that credit should be used sparingly and for things they can afford to pay off. This knowledge can help them avoid credit card debt in the future.

Celebrate Financial Milestones

Celebrating small financial wins encourages them to keep learning. For example, if they reach a savings goal, congratulate them. Positive reinforcement helps them feel good about managing money and motivates them to keep working toward bigger goals.

Simple Ways to Teach Kids About Money

Teaching kids about money from a young age helps them develop good habits that will serve them throughout their lives. By learning to save, spend wisely, and understand the basics of investing, children can grow up with the knowledge they need to make smart financial choices.

Age-Appropriate Lessons on Saving, Spending, and Investing

Teaching kids about money is easiest when you start with simple concepts that match their age and gradually build up. Here are some ways to introduce saving, spending, and investing at different stages:

For Young Children (Ages 3–7)

Young children are naturally curious, so you can start by teaching them the basics of what money is and how it works. At this age, kids learn best through hands-on activities and simple lessons.

Introduce the Concept of Money

Begin by explaining that money is used to buy things. You can use real coins and bills to show them different types of money. Let them touch and feel the coins and bills so they understand that money is something physical and valuable.

Play "Store"

Set up a pretend store at home with toys or snacks, and give your child play money to buy items. This teaches them that money is used for buying things and that it runs out if they spend too much. Playing store is a fun way to introduce spending and budgeting without getting too serious.

Introduce Saving with a Piggy Bank

Give them a piggy bank or jar for saving. Each time they receive a small amount of money, like from a birthday gift or allowance, encourage them to put some of it in the piggy bank. Explain that saving means keeping money for later, so they can buy something special in the future.

Teach Patience with Short-Term Goals

Help them set a small savings goal, like buying a toy or a treat. When they save enough money to buy it, celebrate their achievement. This teaches them patience and the value of saving over time, even for small items.

Explain the Difference Between "Needs" and "Wants"

You can introduce this simple idea by showing that some things, like food and clothes, are needs because we can't live without them, while toys or treats are wants because we can live without them. This helps them understand that money should be used wisely.

For Older Children (Ages 8–12)

As kids get older, they can start learning more about budgeting, planning, and even basic investing. At this age, they understand more complex ideas and can handle small responsibilities with money.

Teach Basic Budgeting with an Allowance

If you give them an allowance, teach them to budget it. For example, they can decide to spend a part of it, save another part, and donate a little to a charity or cause. This helps them understand how to divide money and prioritize spending.

Introduce the Idea of Earning Money

Give them small chores to earn extra money, like helping with household tasks. Earning money helps them understand that it doesn't just appear;

people work to get it. They'll learn to appreciate the effort that goes into making money, and it encourages a strong work ethic.

Use Envelopes or Jars for Budgeting

Give them three envelopes or jars labeled "Save," "Spend," and "Give." Each time they receive money, encourage them to divide it among the jars. The "Save" jar is for bigger goals, the "Spend" jar is for small treats, and the "Give" jar is for donations or gifts. This simple system helps them see where their money is going and teaches them balance.

Set Savings Goals for Bigger Items

If there's something they want, like a video game or a bike, help them set a savings goal and make a plan to reach it. For example, if they need $50, show them how saving $5 a week will get them there in 10 weeks. Tracking their progress helps them stay motivated and teaches them to plan for bigger goals.

Introduce the Concept of Interest with Simple Examples

Explain that when people save money in a bank, they can earn extra money, called interest. You could create a simple game where you add a few extra coins to their savings each month to show how interest works. This teaches them that saving can lead to more money over time.

For Teenagers (Ages 13 and Up)

Teenagers are ready for more detailed lessons on budgeting, earning, and even investing. They may have their own income from part-time jobs, so this is a good time to teach them more about managing money and preparing for the future.

Teach Them to Track Spending

Encourage them to keep track of where their money goes. They can use a notebook or an app to record their expenses. Tracking spending helps them see patterns and teaches them how to manage their money effectively.

Create a Budget for Monthly Expenses

If they have a regular allowance or part-time income, show them how to create a simple monthly budget. Include categories like "Savings,"

"Spending," and "Education" (for books, courses, or school supplies). This helps them practice managing a budget and gives them control over their money.

Explain How Credit Works

Teach them the basics of credit cards and loans. Explain that credit is borrowed money that has to be paid back with extra money (interest). Teach them that it's important to use credit carefully and avoid borrowing more than they can pay back. This understanding helps them avoid common pitfalls with credit in the future.

Introduce Investing with Simple Examples

Show them the basics of investing, like stocks and bonds. Explain that investing is a way to grow money over time. You could use a real-life example, like if they invested $100 in stocks, how that money could grow over years.

Encourage Them to Save for Long-Term Goals

Teenagers can start saving for bigger goals, like college, a car, or travel. Setting long-term goals helps them understand that saving isn't just for small purchases but can also be for future needs. Help them make a plan to reach these goals and teach them about the importance of staying committed.

Encouraging Young People to Develop Healthy Financial Habits Early On

Developing good financial habits is like learning any other skill—it takes time, practice, and patience. Here are ways to encourage healthy money habits in kids and teens:

Be a Good Role Model

Kids learn by watching their parents and adults around them. Show them good habits by budgeting, saving, and spending responsibly. When they see you making careful financial decisions, they're more likely to do the same.

Celebrate Financial Achievements

When they reach a savings goal or make a good financial choice, celebrate their success. Positive reinforcement encourages them to keep practicing good habits. For example, if they save up for a new gadget, praise their effort and commitment.

Teach the Value of Giving

Encourage them to set aside a small portion of their money for donations or gifts. Teaching generosity shows them that money can be used to help others, not just for personal needs. This habit builds empathy and a sense of responsibility toward their community.

Discuss the Importance of Budgeting Regularly

Make budgeting a routine by discussing it with them regularly. Review their budget with them and offer tips. This ongoing practice makes budgeting a natural part of their life and builds confidence in managing money.

Encourage a Savings Mindset

Teach them to think of saving as a priority, not just something they do if they have leftover money. Encourage them to save first and spend what's left. This habit builds a foundation for a secure financial future.

Make Financial Learning Fun and Engaging

Use games, challenges, or even family activities to make financial learning enjoyable. For example, you could have a family saving challenge or play board games that teach financial skills. Fun activities keep kids interested and make learning easier.

Building Generational Wealth

Building generational wealth means creating wealth that can be passed down to your children, grandchildren, and even beyond. It's about making sure that your hard work benefits not only you but also your family's future generations. This chapter covers how to build wealth that lasts and the role of estate planning tools like wills and trusts in protecting that wealth. By planning well, you can give your family a strong financial foundation and help them avoid financial struggles.

How to Build Wealth That Benefits Future Generations

Building wealth that lasts takes time, commitment, and smart planning. Here are some key ways to start building generational wealth:

Investing for the Long Term

Investing is one of the best ways to build wealth over time. When you invest in things like stocks, bonds, or real estate, your money has a chance to grow. Long-term investments usually grow over many years, which can create wealth that lasts for generations.

Stocks and Bonds: Stocks let you own a part of a company, while bonds let you lend money to a company or government in exchange for interest. Over time, stocks tend to grow, and bonds provide steady returns. Investing in a mix of stocks and bonds can create a strong base for generational wealth.

Real Estate: Real estate, like buying a home or rental property, is another great way to build wealth. Real estate often grows in value over time, and rental properties can provide a steady income. Passing down property to future generations gives them a valuable asset they can keep or sell if needed.

Saving and Building an Emergency Fund

Saving is the foundation of financial security. Having money saved protects you from unexpected expenses and gives you a safety net. By saving regularly, you create wealth that can be used in emergencies and doesn't need to be passed down as debt to future generations.

Emergency Fund: An emergency fund is a special savings account that covers unexpected expenses, like car repairs or medical bills. Teaching your children about the importance of saving for emergencies helps them avoid debt and prepares them for unexpected challenges.

Teaching Kids to Save: Passing down healthy saving habits is also a form of wealth. If children learn to save, they're more likely to build their own wealth instead of facing financial problems. Encourage kids to save a part of any money they receive, like an allowance or gifts, to develop good habits.

Starting and Growing a Business

Owning a business can be a powerful way to build wealth. A successful business can create income not only for you but for your children if they choose to continue running it. Many family businesses are passed down from one generation to the next, building a legacy and providing a source of income.

Involving Family Members: If you have a family business, involving your children early on teaches them the value of hard work and how to manage money. This prepares them to take over if they're interested and keeps the business thriving for future generations.

Passing Down Valuable Skills and Knowledge

Sometimes, the best way to build wealth isn't just through money, but by passing down knowledge. Teaching your children about managing money, making smart investments, and budgeting helps them avoid mistakes and grow their wealth. Skills and knowledge are valuable assets that don't lose value over time.

Financial Education: Teach children about finances, including saving, investing, and budgeting. By giving them this knowledge, you're setting them up to manage wealth responsibly, whether it's the money they earn or the wealth they inherit.

The Importance of Estate Planning in Securing Generational Wealth

Once you've built wealth, it's important to protect it and make sure it's passed on according to your wishes. Estate planning is the process of deciding what will happen to your assets after you pass away. Estate planning tools, like wills and trusts, help you control how your wealth is distributed and protect it for future generations. Here's a closer look at these tools:

Wills

A will is a legal document that outlines your wishes for how your assets should be distributed after you pass away. Creating a will is essential for making sure your wealth is passed on to the right people.

Why Wills Matter: Without a will, the government decides how your assets are divided, which may not match your wishes. Having a will ensures that your family receives your assets according to your plan.
Naming Guardians for Children: If you have young children, a will lets you name guardians—people who will take care of them if anything happens to you. This helps protect your children's future and ensures they're cared for by someone you trust.
Keeping Assets in the Family: A will also allows you to choose who receives specific assets, like property, savings, or valuable items. This keeps wealth in the family and allows you to pass down items that may have sentimental value.

Trusts

A trust is a legal arrangement that holds assets for someone's benefit. Trusts offer more control than a will because they let you set rules for how and when assets are distributed. Trusts are especially helpful for managing generational wealth because they can provide long-term protection for your assets.
Benefits of Trusts: Trusts allow you to pass down wealth without going through probate, which is the legal process of distributing assets. This saves time and money for your family and keeps your financial details private.
Setting Conditions: Trusts allow you to set conditions for inheritance. For example, you could arrange for your children to receive a certain amount when they turn 25, 30, and 35 instead of all at once. This can prevent them from spending it too quickly and encourages responsible use of the money.
Protecting Wealth from Taxes and Creditors: Trusts can also protect your assets from taxes and creditors, keeping more of your wealth safe for future generations. Certain types of trusts can help reduce estate taxes, which is the tax on the money and property you pass down. Trusts can also protect assets if your heirs face financial difficulties, ensuring the wealth isn't lost.

Life Insurance

Life insurance provides a payout to your beneficiaries after you pass away. This money can be used to cover living expenses, pay off debts, or invest for the future. Life insurance is especially useful for securing your family's financial future if they rely on your income.

Protecting Family's Lifestyle: Life insurance helps maintain your family's lifestyle and covers basic needs, like housing, education, and health. It gives them time to adjust financially without worrying about immediate expenses.

Using Life Insurance for Wealth Building: Some types of life insurance policies also allow you to build cash value over time. This cash value can be borrowed against or used as a financial resource in emergencies, adding another layer of protection.

Naming Beneficiaries

When you have financial accounts, like retirement accounts or life insurance policies, you can name beneficiaries—people who will receive the money after you pass away. Naming beneficiaries ensures that these assets go directly to the people you choose, skipping the probate process.

Keeping Accounts Up-to-Date: It's important to review your beneficiary designations regularly, especially after big life changes like marriage, divorce, or having children. Keeping this information up-to-date ensures that your wealth goes to the right people.

Setting Up Transfer on Death (TOD) Accounts: Some accounts can be set up as "transfer on death," meaning they automatically go to the named beneficiary without probate. This is a simple way to pass on assets like savings accounts or investments to family members.

Chapter 12

Overcoming Barriers And Building Confidence As A Black Woman Investor

Facing the Unique Challenges Black Women Encounter

Investing can be a powerful way to build wealth, but Black women often face unique challenges in the financial world. From the wealth gap to systemic racism and a lack of representation in financial spaces, these barriers can make it difficult to feel confident and motivated to invest. However, by understanding these challenges and finding strategies to overcome them, Black women can build a path to financial success.

Facing the Unique Challenges Black Women Encounter

There are unique challenges Black women encounter when it comes to building wealth and investing. These challenges are often rooted in systemic issues, which are problems within society that affect certain groups more than others. Here are some of the key challenges Black women may face and how they impact financial success:

The Wealth Gap

The wealth gap refers to the difference in wealth between groups of people. In the United States, Black families generally have less wealth compared to white families. This gap is influenced by many factors, including lower average wages, limited access to wealth-building resources, and historical discrimination. Because of the wealth gap, many Black women may start their financial journey with fewer resources, making it harder to invest and build wealth.

For example, if someone doesn't have extra money saved, they may find it challenging to invest, even though investing could help them grow their wealth. The wealth gap can make it harder to start, but it's important to know that even small steps can make a difference over time. Investing small amounts consistently is a good way to get started, even if the amount seems small at first.

Systemic Racism

Systemic racism includes policies and practices that disadvantage people based on race. In financial spaces, this can mean that Black women may not have the same access to opportunities or support as others. For example, they might be less likely to receive loans, find mentors, or be encouraged to explore financial options like investing.

Systemic racism can also lead to feelings of exclusion or isolation in financial environments. When people don't see others who look like them in these spaces, it can create a feeling of being an outsider. However, knowing that these barriers exist can help Black women find strategies to overcome them, such as connecting with diverse financial communities.

Lack of Representation in Financial Spaces

Financial industries often lack diversity, meaning there are few Black women represented in roles like financial advisors, investment managers, and other positions of influence. This lack of representation can make it harder for Black women to see themselves in these fields and feel confident about entering them.

Representation matters because it shows people that they, too, can achieve financial success. When Black women don't see themselves represented, it can create doubt about whether investing is "for them." Finding role models, mentors, or supportive networks with people from similar backgrounds can help build confidence and create a sense of belonging in the financial world.

Strategies for Overcoming These Barriers and Creating Your Own Path to Financial Success

Despite the challenges, there are ways to overcome these barriers and build a successful path in investing. Here are some strategies that can help Black women take control of their finances, grow their confidence, and achieve their financial goals.

Start with Financial Education

Financial education is the foundation of investing success. Learning about topics like budgeting, saving, investing, and debt management can empower Black women to make informed financial decisions. There are many resources available, including books, online courses, and workshops that provide clear, practical information.

Find Trusted Resources: Start by looking for financial resources created by diverse experts or organizations that understand the unique challenges Black women face. Books like "The Wealth Choice" by Dr. Dennis Kimbro or podcasts led by Black financial advisors offer relatable advice that can build financial knowledge.

Use Free or Low-Cost Tools: Many financial resources, like budgeting apps or educational websites, are free or inexpensive. These tools can help make managing money easier without requiring a big financial commitment.

Build a Supportive Network

Creating a network of supportive people who understand the journey toward financial success can make a big difference. Connecting with other Black women who are also interested in investing or financial growth can provide motivation, encouragement, and valuable information.

Join Financial Groups and Communities: There are many groups, both online and offline, where Black women can connect to discuss investing and finances. Groups like these can offer advice, share resources, and provide support. Finding a community of people with similar goals can make the journey feel less isolated.

Find a Mentor or Financial Advisor: Mentors or advisors can offer guidance on specific financial goals, answer questions, and give personalized advice.

Some organizations, such as the Association of African American Financial Advisors (AAAA), can help connect Black women with advisors who understand their unique experiences.

Set Clear Financial Goals

Setting specific financial goals can help focus your efforts and provide motivation. Goals make it easier to track progress and adjust as needed. For example, you might set a goal to save $500 in an emergency fund or invest a certain amount each month.

Break Down Big Goals into Small Steps: Big goals can feel overwhelming, so breaking them down into smaller, manageable steps can make them more achievable. For example, if your goal is to save for a down payment on a house, set smaller goals, like saving a certain amount each month.

Celebrate Small Wins: Recognize and celebrate each milestone, no matter how small. Reaching smaller goals can build confidence and help you stay motivated for the bigger ones.

Start Investing with Small Amounts

It's a common misconception that investing requires a lot of money upfront. In reality, many platforms allow people to start investing with small amounts, making it accessible to more people. Investing, even with small amounts, is a great way to begin building wealth over time.

Explore Low-Cost Investment Options: Many apps, like Robinhood or Acorns, allow you to start investing with as little as $5. These platforms make it easy to learn the basics of investing without needing a large sum of money.

Consider Long-Term Investments: Long-term investments, like index funds or mutual funds, tend to grow steadily over time. They're a good option for beginners because they don't require daily monitoring, which can make investing feel more manageable.

Build Financial Confidence Through Education and Action

Confidence in investing often grows with knowledge and experience. The more you learn and practice, the more comfortable you'll feel making

financial decisions. Start by taking small actions, like creating a budget, setting savings goals, or investing a small amount, and build from there.
Learn from Mistakes: Everyone makes mistakes, especially when learning something new. View mistakes as learning experiences that can make you a better investor. Reflect on what happened, adjust your approach, and keep moving forward.
Stay Informed: The financial world is always changing, and staying updated on trends, news, and changes can help you make informed choices. Subscribe to a financial newsletter or follow reliable sources to keep learning and growing your knowledge.

Advocate for Financial Inclusion and Representation

Advocating for representation and inclusion in financial spaces helps create change that benefits everyone. Supporting businesses, advisors, and financial institutions that promote diversity can make financial services more welcoming and accessible to Black women and others.
Support Diverse Financial Experts: Many Black financial advisors, authors, and speakers are working to make financial literacy more accessible. Supporting these experts not only helps them but also promotes a more inclusive financial community.
Encourage Open Conversations About Money: Money can be a sensitive topic, but talking openly about it can help remove stigma and encourage others to learn. Having conversations about money with family, friends, or colleagues can make financial topics feel more normal and less intimidating.

Building Confidence as an Investor

Investing can feel uncertain, especially when you're just starting. Building confidence as an investor takes time, patience, and a willingness to learn. Confidence doesn't mean you'll never make mistakes; it means trusting yourself to make informed decisions, learning from those mistakes, and continuing to grow.

How to Trust Your Instincts in Investing

Trusting your instincts means learning to listen to your inner voice when making financial choices. Instincts develop over time, especially as you gain experience and knowledge. Here are some ways to build trust in your instincts as an investor:

Start Small and Build Gradually

Starting small allows you to take less risk and learn as you go. For example, you might start by investing a small amount in a familiar stock or a basic mutual fund. Over time, as you see how your investments grow (or sometimes decrease), you gain experience. This experience helps you feel more comfortable making larger decisions in the future.

Learn the Basics First

It's easier to trust your instincts when you understand what you're investing in. Learning basic concepts like stocks, bonds, and interest rates can give you a strong foundation. Once you understand the basics, you'll have a better idea of how different investments work, which can help you make decisions with more confidence.

Take Time to Reflect

Before making any big investment, take a moment to think it through. Ask yourself why you want to make this investment and what you expect from it. Sometimes, the initial excitement of an investment can leads to quick decisions, so taking a step back helps you make a calm, thoughtful choice. Trust grows when you know you've made choices after careful reflection.

Learn from Each Decision

Each investment, whether successful or not, teaches you something valuable. If an investment doesn't work out, don't view it as a failure. Instead, look at it as a learning opportunity. Ask yourself what you could do differently next time. Learning from each choice helps you understand your instincts better, so you can trust them more over time.

Developing Financial Discipline

Financial discipline means staying focused on your goals, managing your money wisely, and avoiding impulsive decisions. Discipline is important because it keeps you on track even when investing feels uncertain or tempting. Here are some ways to develop financial discipline as an investor:

Set Clear Investment Goals

Clear goals help you stay focused. For example, you might set a goal to save for retirement, buy a home, or build an emergency fund. By knowing exactly what you're working toward, it's easier to make disciplined choices that support your goals.

Create a Budget for Investing

Set a specific amount of money you're comfortable investing each month. This keeps your investing in balance with other financial needs, like paying bills or saving for emergencies. Sticking to a budget prevents you from over-investing or making impulsive decisions based on excitement.

Stay Patient and Avoid Quick Gains

Sometimes, people get excited about investments that promise quick returns, but these are often risky. Developing discipline means being patient and focusing on long-term growth. Remind yourself that investing is a journey, not a race. Long-term investments tend to grow steadily, helping you reach your goals without taking unnecessary risks.

Review Your Investments Regularly

Regularly checking in on your investments helps you stay disciplined. Set a specific time each month to review your investment performance. This practice gives you a chance to make adjustments if needed and keeps you aware of your progress, helping you stay committed to your goals.

Control Emotions in Decision-Making

It's normal to feel emotional about money, but emotional decisions can lead to mistakes. For example, when the stock market drops, it's easy to feel nervous and want to sell. However, staying calm and focusing on your long-term plan is usually the best approach. Developing financial discipline helps you make thoughtful choices rather than reacting to emotions.

Staying Informed About Your Investments

Knowledge is power when it comes to investing. Staying informed helps you make better decisions, feel more confident, and avoid potential risks. Here's how to stay updated and informed about your investments:

Read Reliable Financial News

Staying informed about financial news can give you insights into how the market works and current trends. Look for trusted sources like financial news websites, newspapers, or newsletters. Reading a little each day or week helps you build a habit of staying informed.

Use Educational Resources

There are many resources, like books, online courses, and podcasts, that provide valuable information for investors. These resources cover topics like stocks, bonds, real estate, and more. As you learn, you'll feel more comfortable and confident in making investment choices.

Keep Track of Market Trends

Markets go through cycles of highs and lows. By keeping track of these trends, you can better understand when it's a good time to buy or hold. However, remember that staying informed doesn't mean making frequent changes; it's about being aware and using that knowledge to support your long-term goals.

Understand Your Portfolio

A portfolio is the collection of all your investments. Review it regularly to make sure your investments are balanced and aligned with your goals. For example, if one stock has grown a lot, it might now make up a big part of your portfolio, so you might want to adjust it. Knowing what's in your portfolio gives you control and confidence.

Ask Questions

Don't hesitate to ask questions, whether it's from a mentor, a financial advisor, or even through online resources. Asking questions helps you understand your choices better, giving you more confidence. Learning is an ongoing process, and questions are a natural part of it.

The Importance of Surrounding Yourself with Supportive Networks and Mentors

Having a strong support network makes a big difference in building confidence as an investor. Surrounding yourself with people who share similar goals, have experience, or offer encouragement can provide the motivation you need to stay on track. Here's how supportive networks and mentors can help:

Connecting with Like-Minded People

Joining groups or communities of people who are also interested in investing helps you learn from each other's experiences. These groups can be online or in-person and provide a place to discuss ideas, share tips, and offer support. Being part of a community keeps you motivated and makes the process more enjoyable.

Finding Mentors Who Guide You

A mentor is someone with experience who can offer advice and guidance. Mentors can help you make smart decisions, avoid mistakes, and build confidence. For example, if you're unsure about a particular investment, a mentor can help you think it through based on their own experiences.

Learning from Others' Experiences

Sometimes, the best lessons come from others' experiences. By talking to other investors, you can learn about their successes and mistakes. Learning from their stories helps you avoid similar mistakes and gives you new ideas to try. Every conversation is an opportunity to gain knowledge and build your own confidence.

Encouragement During Difficult Times

The market can be unpredictable, and there may be times when you feel discouraged or unsure. Having a support network means you can share these feelings with others who understand. Encouragement from others reminds you that everyone faces challenges, and it's okay to feel uncertain sometimes. A supportive network can give you the boost you need to keep going.

Building Accountability

Being part of a group or having a mentor creates a sense of accountability, meaning you feel motivated to stick to your goals. For example, if you set a goal to invest a certain amount each month, sharing this goal with your group can help you stay committed. Knowing others are rooting for you makes it easier to stay on track.

Celebrating Success Together

Celebrating successes, big or small, is essential for building confidence. When you reach a financial milestone, like saving a certain amount or seeing your investment grow, share it with your network. Celebrating together helps you feel proud of your progress and encourages you to keep aiming higher.

Celebrating Your Success

Reaching financial goals is an accomplishment worth celebrating. Recognizing your own success helps keep you motivated to reach even higher, and it reinforces your commitment to your financial journey. Along with celebrating personal achievements, giving back to your community and inspiring others—especially other Black women—adds deeper meaning to your success. This chapter discusses the value of recognizing your accomplishments, staying motivated, and making a positive impact by encouraging others to invest and grow financially.

Recognizing Your Accomplishments and Staying Motivated

Reaching financial milestones, big or small, deserves to be celebrated. Whether you've saved a certain amount, paid off a debt, or made your first successful investment, these achievements are stepping stones toward financial freedom. Here's why recognizing your progress is essential and some ways to celebrate:

Building Confidence

Every time you reach a financial goal, you build confidence. It shows that you're capable of managing money wisely and that you can achieve what you set out to do. Celebrating each accomplishment, even the small ones, helps reinforce that you're on the right path and encourages you to keep going.

For example, if you set a goal to save $500 and reach it, take a moment to feel proud. This sense of pride is a powerful motivator that builds your belief in your abilities, making you more willing to set and achieve larger goals in the future.

Keeping Up Momentum

Financial goals often take time, and it's easy to lose motivation along the way. Recognizing your progress keeps you energized. By celebrating small steps, you're more likely to stay committed to your long-term goals because you see that each milestone is bringing you closer to success.

For example, if you're working toward paying off debt, each payment you make is a step closer to freedom from debt. Celebrate these small steps by acknowledging your progress, which keeps you focused on your ultimate goal of being debt-free.

Setting New Goals

Celebrating a completed goal gives you a natural point to reflect and think about what you want to achieve next. Financial success is often a journey with many goals along the way. After reaching one milestone, set a new one that challenges you a bit further. This way, you keep growing, learning, and pushing yourself to do more.

For example, after building an emergency fund, you might set a goal to start investing. Each goal you reach and celebrate builds a foundation for the next one, helping you progress steadily toward financial freedom.

Creating Positive Associations with Money

For many people, money can feel stressful or difficult. By celebrating financial wins, you're creating positive feelings around money, which helps reduce fear and anxiety. Instead of focusing on challenges, you begin to see money as something that brings growth and opportunity.

If you see money as a tool that helps you reach goals and feel proud of your achievements, it becomes easier to manage finances with confidence. These positive associations can lead to healthier financial habits over time.

Ways to Celebrate Your Financial Success

Celebration doesn't have to be grand or expensive. Here are some meaningful ways to acknowledge your financial achievements:

Treat Yourself to Something Small

Reward yourself with something that makes you happy but doesn't take away from your financial progress. For example, you could enjoy a nice meal, buy a book you've wanted, or take a day off to relax. Small rewards remind you of your progress without undoing your hard work.

Share Your Achievement with Loved Ones

Sharing your success with family or friends who support your goals can make the celebration more meaningful. Their encouragement can boost your confidence and make you feel proud of what you've accomplished. Celebrating with others who believe in you reminds you that you're not alone on this journey.

Write Down Your Achievements

Keeping a journal of your financial successes is a great way to see how far you've come. When you face challenges, looking back at past accomplishments can remind you of your ability to succeed. Writing down your achievements helps keep them fresh in your mind and reinforces your confidence.

Take Time to Reflect on Your Progress

Reflection is a powerful tool for growth. After reaching a goal, take some time to think about what worked well, what you learned, and how you can continue making progress. Reflecting on your journey helps you appreciate the steps you've taken and gives you insights to apply to future goals.

The Importance of Giving Back to Your Community

As you grow financially, giving back to your community can make your success even more meaningful. Supporting others, especially other Black women who may face similar challenges, can create positive change and help build wealth for future generations. Here's why giving back is important and some ways to do it:

Building Stronger Communities

When successful individuals give back, they help create opportunities for others. This can mean sharing knowledge, offering support, or providing financial resources to help others reach their goals. Strong communities are built on support and encouragement, and each person who gives back contributes to a better future for everyone.

For example, donating to organizations that support financial literacy for Black women can help others gain the skills they need to succeed. By giving back, you're strengthening the community and helping others achieve their goals.

Inspiring Future Generations

When younger people see others who look like them achieving financial success, it inspires them to believe they can do the same. Representation matters, and by giving back, you're showing others that financial success is possible for them too. This positive influence can make a big difference in encouraging more Black women to invest and build wealth.

For instance, mentoring young women who are interested in finance or starting a business shows them that they have support and guidance. Sharing your own journey can inspire them to set goals and pursue their dreams with confidence.

Creating a Legacy of Wealth and Support

Generational wealth isn't just about money; it's also about knowledge and support. By giving back, you're helping build a legacy that benefits your community for years to come. Teaching others about money, investing, or business helps ensure that future generations have the tools they need for financial success.

For example, hosting financial workshops or sharing investment tips with others can create a ripple effect. Each person who learns from you can then pass that knowledge on, creating a lasting impact that strengthens the community.

Ways to Give Back and Inspire Others

Giving back can take many forms. Here are some ways to make a positive impact and encourage other Black women to invest and grow financially:

Mentoring and Sharing Knowledge

Mentorship is a powerful way to support others. By mentoring someone who is interested in investing or financial growth, you can share valuable insights, answer questions, and help them feel more confident. Mentorship doesn't have to be formal; even a few conversations can make a big difference.

For example, if you know someone who wants to start investing, offer to meet up and share what you've learned. Helping others feel confident about their first steps can encourage them to keep learning and growing.

Supporting Black-Owned Businesses

Supporting Black-owned businesses helps build economic strength within the community. By buying from Black-owned companies or investing in them, you're helping create jobs, opportunities, and financial stability. This support benefits both the business owners and the larger community.

Volunteering with Financial Education Programs

Many organizations offer financial education programs aimed at helping people learn about money, budgeting, and investing. Volunteering with these programs allows you to share your knowledge and support others on their financial journey. Programs like these are often eager for volunteers who can relate to their audiences.

Starting or Joining Financial Support Groups

Support groups provide a space for people to share goals, challenges, and successes. Starting or joining a financial support group for Black women can create a community where people feel safe discussing their financial journeys. Group members can share advice, motivate each other, and celebrate each other's successes.

Creating Content to Share Financial Knowledge

If you enjoy writing, creating videos, or sharing on social media, consider sharing what you've learned about investing and finances. Content like blog posts, videos, or social media posts can reach a wide audience and inspire others to start their own financial journey. Seeing relatable content from someone with a similar background can motivate others to learn and grow.

Chapter 13

Creating A Long-Term Investment Strategy

Thinking Long-Term

Creating a long-term investment strategy is about making a plan to grow your money over many years. It's one of the best ways to build lasting wealth because it lets your money grow steadily without getting caught up in short-term risks. When you focus on the long term, you give your investments the chance to grow through the power of compounding, which is when your returns earn more returns over time.

Why Long-Term Investing is Important for Building Wealth

Long-term investing has several advantages that make it a great way to build wealth. Here's why focusing on the long term is important:

Compounding Growth Over Time

Compounding is when you earn returns not only on the money you originally invested but also on the returns you've already made. For example, if you invest $1,000 and it grows by 7% each year, after 10 years, your investment will have grown significantly, not just from the original amount, but from the returns it generated over time.

The longer you invest, the more compounding helps your money grow. This "growth on growth" effect is one of the most powerful benefits of long-term investing. Even small investments can become large amounts if they have enough time to grow.

Reduced Impact of Market Ups and Downs

The stock market and other types of investments go up and down regularly, which can make short-term investing risky. When you invest for the long term, you don't have to worry as much about these daily ups and downs.

Over many years, investments often recover from short-term losses and continue to grow.

For example, if the market drops for a few months, a long-term investor knows that the market usually recovers over time. Staying invested for many years helps reduce the stress of market drops because you're focused on the bigger picture, not just what happens in the short term.

Lower Investment Costs

Long-term investors typically buy and hold their investments rather than buying and selling frequently. This "buy and hold" approach helps reduce costs, such as transaction fees or taxes on profits, which can add up if you trade often.

By holding onto your investments for the long term, you avoid these extra costs, which means more of your money stays invested and keeps growing. This approach is not only simpler but also more cost-effective, making it an ideal way to build wealth over time.

Great for Reaching Big Financial Goals

Long-term investing is perfect for achieving large financial goals, like saving for retirement, buying a house, or funding education. These goals require big amounts of money, and long-term investing gives you the time needed to grow your funds.

For example, if you start investing in your 20s with the goal of retiring in your 60s, your investments will have around 40 years to grow. This long timeline allows for steady growth, meaning you can reach big financial goals with smaller contributions that grow over time.

Avoids the Pressure of "Timing the Market"

Trying to "time the market" means guessing the best times to buy or sell investments to make a quick profit. This can be challenging and stressful, even for experienced investors. Long-term investing helps you avoid this pressure because you stay invested no matter what happens in the market. By focusing on the long-term growth of your investments, you don't need to worry about buying or selling at the "perfect" moment. This approach makes investing simpler and more reliable, allowing you to focus on your financial goals rather than reacting to market changes.

Staying Focused on Your Goals and Avoiding Emotional Decisions

Even with a strong long-term plan, it's natural to feel nervous when markets change. Market ups and downs can make you want to react quickly, but making decisions based on emotions can hurt your long-term progress. Here are some strategies to help you stay focused on your goals and avoid emotional choices:

Set Clear Investment Goals

Knowing what you're working toward helps you stay committed to your investment plan. Goals give your investments a purpose, such as saving for retirement, buying a home, or building an emergency fund. Clear goals remind you why you're investing and keep you motivated, even when markets are uncertain.

For instance, if your goal is to retire comfortably, you can remind yourself that the purpose of your investments is long-term growth, not short-term gains. Focusing on your goals helps you stay steady, even when the market fluctuates.

Create a Diversified Portfolio

Diversification means spreading your investments across different types of assets, like stocks, bonds, and real estate, rather than putting all your money in one place. A diversified portfolio helps reduce risk because if one investment doesn't do well, others can balance it out.

For example, if you invest in both stocks and bonds, your portfolio might not lose as much value when the stock market is down because bonds tend to be more stable. Diversification makes your investments more stable, which helps you stay calm and committed during market changes.

Avoid Checking Your Investments Too Often

Constantly checking your investments can lead to stress, especially when you see your balance go up and down. Instead, set specific times to review your investments, like once a month or every few months. This way, you're less likely to make decisions based on short-term changes.

By checking less often, you focus more on long-term progress and less on daily fluctuations. This habit makes it easier to stick to your plan and stay confident in your strategy.

Focus on Long-Term Growth, Not Quick Gains

Long-term investing is about allowing your money to grow steadily over time, rather than trying to make quick gains. Remember that big financial goals, like retirement or buying a home, require patience and steady growth, not quick profits.

For example, by investing in a diverse portfolio and letting it grow over the years, you're more likely to reach your goals. Focusing on long-term growth helps you avoid risky decisions that may promise quick returns but could also lead to losses.

Stay Prepared for Market Fluctuations

It's helpful to have a plan for when markets drop or rise sharply. Knowing that markets go up and down, prepare yourself to stay invested even during difficult times. This way, you're ready and don't feel pressured to make quick decisions based on emotions.

When you have a plan, you feel more in control of your investments. This confidence helps you stick to your goals and avoid emotional reactions when the market fluctuates.

Learn from Successful Long-Term Investors

Many successful investors have used a long-term approach to build their wealth. Learning from their stories can be inspiring and show you the value of patience and steady growth. Famous long-term investors like Warren Buffett have shared advice that can help you feel confident in a long-term strategy.

These investors often recommend focusing on quality investments and giving them time to grow rather than trying to make quick gains. Reading about their experiences and following their advice can remind you that long-term investing works, even when markets are volatile.

Reviewing and Adjusting Your Portfolio

Reviewing and adjusting your portfolio means regularly checking your investments and making changes if needed. This is important because our financial needs and goals can change over time. By reviewing your portfolio, you ensure that your investments still match your goals and keep you on the path to financial success.

Why Regularly Reviewing Your Investments Matters

As time goes on, our financial needs can shift. You might start with one goal, like saving for a home, but later focus more on retirement or funding education. Life changes—such as a new job, marriage, children, or retirement—can also affect your financial goals. When you review your portfolio regularly, you ensure that your investments match your current priorities. By doing so, you avoid the risk of having money tied up in things that no longer suit your needs.

Another reason to review your portfolio is to keep track of how your investments are performing. Some investments may grow well, while others might lose value or not meet your expectations. By checking regularly, you can decide if certain investments are helping you reach your goals or if they need adjustment. This regular review helps you stay in control and make decisions that keep your money working effectively.

How Often Should You Review Your Portfolio?

A good rule is to review your portfolio at least once a year. This gives you a clear picture of how your investments are doing and if they're aligned with your goals. Some people prefer to check more often, like every six months, to stay updated. However, avoid checking too frequently, like every week, as short-term changes can be distracting and lead to unnecessary stress. Remember, investments are meant to grow over time, and short-term ups and downs are normal.

If there's a big change in your life, such as a new job, a major purchase, or a family addition, it can also be a good time to review your portfolio. Life changes often mean adjustments in your financial needs, so checking your investments after big events helps you stay on track with your new goals.

Steps to Review Your Portfolio

When reviewing your portfolio, follow these steps to make the process simple and effective:

1. Check Your Investment Performance

Start by looking at how each investment is doing. Are your stocks, bonds, or mutual funds meeting your expectations? Compare the growth of each investment to similar ones to see if they're performing well. For example, if you own stock in a company, check how it's doing compared to others in the same industry. If your investments are underperforming, think about whether they still have potential or if it might be time to replace them with better options.

2. Evaluate Your Goals

Next, think about your current financial goals. Are you still focused on retirement, or have your priorities shifted? If your goals have changed, adjust your portfolio to match them. For example, if you're closer to retirement, you may want to focus more on safer investments, like bonds, instead of riskier ones like stocks. Adjusting based on your goals helps ensure that your portfolio is always working toward what matters most to you.

3. Check Your Asset Allocation

Asset allocation is how you divide your investments across different categories, like stocks, bonds, and real estate. A balanced allocation helps reduce risk because it spreads your money across different types of assets. Over time, however, your allocation can shift as some investments grow faster than others. For instance, if your stocks grow significantly, they may make up a larger part of your portfolio than you intended. Reviewing your allocation helps you see if your portfolio is still balanced or if adjustments are needed.

4. Consider Any Fees or Costs

Some investments come with fees, like management fees for mutual funds or transaction fees for certain accounts. These costs can add up over time and reduce your returns. During your review, check if the fees are reasonable or if you could find similar investments with lower costs. Lower fees mean more of your money stays invested, which helps it grow faster.

5. Look at Your Investment's Risk Level

Different investments come with different levels of risk. When you first created your portfolio, you likely chose a level of risk that suited your goals and comfort level. Over time, your comfort with risk may change, especially as you get closer to reaching a financial goal. Reviewing your portfolio allows you to adjust the risk level if needed, either by adding safer investments or removing higher-risk ones.

When and How to Rebalance Your Portfolio

Rebalancing your portfolio means adjusting your investments to return to your original allocation. For example, if you wanted your portfolio to be 60% stocks and 40% bonds, but your stocks have grown to make up 70%, you might sell some stocks or buy more bonds to get back to your 60/40 target. Rebalancing helps keep your portfolio aligned with your risk tolerance and goals.

Set a Schedule for Rebalancing

Many investors choose to rebalance once a year, while others prefer doing it every six months. Setting a schedule helps you stay consistent without needing to watch the market constantly. A yearly or twice-a-year rebalance ensures that your portfolio stays on track without being affected by every short-term change.

Use Rebalancing as a Time to Adjust Goals

Rebalancing is a good time to revisit your goals. For example, if you're getting closer to retirement, you may want to shift toward more conservative investments, like bonds or cash, rather than stocks. This adjustment helps protect your money as you near your goal. Similarly, if your risk tolerance has changed, rebalancing allows you to adjust your portfolio to better match your comfort level.

Know When to Add or Remove Investments

During your review, you may notice that certain investments no longer match your goals or are underperforming. If an investment isn't helping you reach your goals, it might be time to replace it with one that has more potential. Adding new investments can also be a good idea if you find opportunities that better fit your strategy.

For example, if you see a new mutual fund that offers good growth potential and fits your risk level, you might choose to add it to your portfolio. Just remember to balance each addition with the rest of your investments to maintain your desired allocation.

Stay Disciplined and Avoid Emotional Reactions

When markets fluctuate, it's easy to feel tempted to make quick changes to your portfolio. However, rebalancing is best done in a disciplined, planned way rather than as a reaction to market changes. By rebalancing based on your set schedule and goals, you avoid the risk of making emotional decisions that may hurt your long-term plan.

Staying calm and following a strategy helps you make thoughtful decisions, keeping your portfolio focused on steady growth. Avoiding emotional reactions protects you from the mistakes that can come from acting on impulse, ensuring that your portfolio serves your long-term interests.

Building a Legacy of Wealth

Building a legacy of wealth means creating financial security that can benefit not just yourself but also your children, grandchildren, and future generations. This is more than just saving money; it's about making smart financial choices that will provide your family with stability and opportunities long after you're gone. When you build a legacy of wealth, you leave a foundation that can help your loved ones achieve their own goals and dreams.

How Your Investment Journey Can Create a Legacy for Future Generations

Your investment journey is the path you take to grow and manage your money. With smart and careful investing, you can build wealth that lasts beyond your own lifetime. Here's how your investments today can create a legacy that benefits future generations:

Growing Wealth Over Time with Investments

Investments, like stocks, bonds, and real estate, grow over time. As you invest in these assets, your wealth increases not only for yourself but also for the generations that come after you. When you leave your investments to your children or grandchildren, they inherit a strong financial foundation. They can use this money to fund their education, start a business, or buy a home.

For example, if you invest in a retirement account or stocks and leave them untouched, they can grow significantly over several decades. This growth creates a pool of wealth that future generations can rely on, providing them with financial security and options that they might not have had otherwise.

Setting an Example of Financial Responsibility

By investing and managing money wisely, you set an example for your family. When they see you saving, investing, and making thoughtful financial choices, they learn to do the same. Teaching your children and grandchildren about managing money responsibly is one of the best ways to ensure they will continue building on the wealth you pass down.

Setting an example includes talking openly about saving, investing, and avoiding debt. By showing them how to make smart financial decisions, you give them the tools they need to continue building wealth, which helps create a long-lasting legacy.

Creating a Family Tradition of Wealth Building

Some families pass down traditions, like certain foods, skills, or values. Similarly, you can create a tradition of wealth building by encouraging each generation to invest and save wisely. When building wealth becomes a family priority, it helps ensure that future generations have financial security and opportunities to succeed.

You can start by involving your children in simple financial activities, like budgeting or saving for a goal. As they get older, teach them about investments and how to grow their money. This tradition of wealth building makes it more likely that your family will continue to prosper for many years.

Leaving Behind Assets That Can Continue to Grow

Some assets, like real estate or certain stocks, can continue to grow in value over time. Leaving these assets to your heirs not only provides them with money but also with investments that can keep growing. For instance, if you leave a property to your family, they can benefit from its value increasing over the years or from rental income if they choose to rent it out.

Leaving assets that can grow also gives your family a financial safety net. It provides them with options, whether they choose to use the asset for their needs or let it continue to grow. This helps them build on your wealth rather than starting from scratch, making your legacy more secure and lasting.

Encouraging Long-Term Thinking in Your Financial and Personal Life

Creating a legacy of wealth requires a focus on long-term thinking. This means planning not just for your immediate needs but for the future. Long-term thinking is important for both financial success and for creating a legacy that benefits future generations. Here's how you can practice and encourage long-term thinking:

Setting Long-Term Financial Goals

Long-term financial goals, like saving for retirement, buying a home, or creating an education fund for your children, help you stay focused on the future. By setting and working toward these goals, you create a roadmap for building wealth over time. These goals guide your financial choices and make sure you're always moving forward.

For example, saving for retirement from an early age gives your money time to grow, which results in a larger amount by the time you're ready to retire.

This long-term growth supports both you and your family, as it reduces the financial burden on future generations.

Building a Legacy Through Education

Education is one of the most valuable gifts you can leave for future generations. Teaching your family about money and how to make smart financial choices ensures they have the knowledge to continue building wealth. You can share lessons on budgeting, saving, investing, and even setting financial goals.

Teaching financial skills empowers your children to make wise choices, allowing them to carry on your legacy. This education can be as simple as explaining how a savings account works or as detailed as teaching them about different types of investments. With this knowledge, they're more likely to grow the wealth you leave behind.

Practicing Patience and Consistency

Long-term thinking requires patience and consistency. Building wealth doesn't happen overnight; it's the result of regular savings, wise investments, and disciplined choices over many years. Practicing patience in your investment journey shows your family that staying committed and focused leads to success.

For instance, investing a small amount consistently each month adds up over the years. The discipline to keep investing, even when it seems slow, teaches the importance of perseverance. This lesson is valuable for wealth building and for achieving any life goal.

Protecting Wealth with Proper Planning

Protecting your wealth is as important as building it. Estate planning, which includes creating a will and possibly setting up trusts, ensures that your assets are distributed according to your wishes. This planning helps avoid potential issues, like legal fees or taxes, that could reduce the amount your family receives.

Proper planning protects your family's financial future by making the transfer of wealth smooth and efficient. For example, a trust can specify how and when your heirs receive their inheritance, ensuring that the wealth is used responsibly and lasts for a long time.

Encouraging Family Values of Responsibility and Generosity

Long-term wealth building goes hand-in-hand with strong family values, like responsibility and generosity. Teaching your family to use wealth wisely and to help others when possible creates a legacy that's not just about money but also about positive impact. Generosity can include helping others in your family or giving back to your community.

When your family values financial responsibility and kindness, they're more likely to use their wealth in meaningful ways that honor your legacy. This approach helps them appreciate the wealth you pass down, using it to improve their lives and make a positive difference in the world.

The Lasting Impact of a Wealth Legacy

Leaving a legacy of wealth is about more than just passing down money. It's about giving your family a head start, helping them reach their goals, and teaching them to be financially responsible. When you create a strong financial foundation, you help future generations avoid the struggles that can come with financial instability. This foundation allows them to focus on growth, learning, and making choices that improve their lives.

Conclusion

Finally, we started by learning what investing is and how it can help you grow your wealth over time. We discussed setting clear financial goals, creating a simple plan, and choosing investments that fit your needs. You've also learned about different types of investments like stocks, bonds, and real estate, and how each one can help you reach your goals.

One of the key lessons is that investing isn't just for people with lots of money or special knowledge. It's for everyone, and anyone can start investing, even with a small amount. You don't need to be an expert or have a lot of money to take your first step. In fact, every dollar you invest today brings you closer to financial freedom tomorrow. Small steps, like opening an investment account or saving a few dollars each month, are powerful because they add up over time.

Another big lesson is about confidence. Many people feel nervous about investing because they don't trust themselves to make the right choices. But investing doesn't have to be perfect to be effective. It's okay to start small and learn as you go. By taking action and making small steps, you'll become more comfortable with investing. Building wealth is a journey, and each decision you make helps you grow more confident and knowledgeable. Mistakes may happen, but they're just part of the learning process. The key is to keep going and to keep learning.

Throughout, we've also talked about the importance of being patient and sticking with your plan. Building wealth takes time. There may be moments when the market goes up or down, and it's easy to feel worried. But staying focused on your goals and trusting the process will help you reach financial freedom. Investing is like planting a garden—you won't see results right away, but with patience and care, it will grow. Over time, the small amounts you invest can become a secure foundation that supports you and your family.

By investing and making smart money choices, you're not just securing your own future but also creating something lasting for future generations. You're building a strong foundation that can give your children and grandchildren more opportunities and financial security. This is a powerful gift, and it's something that can make a difference for years to come.

Trust yourself, take that first step, and don't be afraid to learn as you go. Every investment, every dollar saved, and every smart choice brings you closer to financial freedom. Building wealth takes time, patience, and effort, but the results are worth it. Imagine the freedom of having choices, security, and a life where money worries don't hold you back.

So, start your investment journey today with confidence. Trust in yourself, follow the lessons you've learned, and keep moving forward, one step at a time. You can do this, and the future you dream of is within reach. Remember, each small action you take brings you closer to a stronger, more secure financial future. Invest with confidence you have everything it takes to succeed.

Made in the USA
Monee, IL
04 November 2026

67381345R00095